The Fair Trade Revolution

KEEP IN TOUCH WITH PLUTO PRESS

For special offers, author updates, new title info and more there are plenty of ways to stay in touch with Pluto Press.

Our Website: http://www.plutobooks.com

Our Blog: http://plutopress.wordpress.com

Our Facebook: http://www.facebook.com/PlutoPress

Our Twitter: http://twitter.com/plutopress

PlutoPress
www.plutobooks.com

The Fair Trade Revolution

Edited by
John Bowes

PlutoPress
www.plutobooks.com

First published 2011 by Pluto Press
345 Archway Road, London N6 5AA and
175 Fifth Avenue, New York, NY 10010

www.plutobooks.com

Distributed in the United States of America exclusively by
Palgrave Macmillan, a division of St. Martin's Press LLC,
175 Fifth Avenue, New York, NY 10010

British Library Cataloguing in Publication Data
A catalogue record for this book is available from the British Library

ISBN   978 0 7453 3079 2   Hardback
ISBN   978 0 7453 3078 5   Paperback

Library of Congress Cataloging in Publication Data applied for

10   9   8   7   6   5   4   3   2   1

Designed and produced for Pluto Press by
Chase Publishing Services Ltd, 33 Livonia Road, Sidmouth, EX10 9JB, England
Typeset from disk by Stanford DTP Services, Northampton, England
Printed and bound in the European Union by
CPI Antony Rowe, Chippenham and Eastbourne

Contents

Foreword

A few decades ago some pioneering individuals and organisations decided to put their values into practice with the development of something called 'fair trade'. This book provides an insightful and important analysis of the development of the fair trade movement worldwide, built around the experiences and perspectives of several of the key individuals who led the way. As we reflect on the most important trends in business of the twentieth century, we certainly must include the expansion of fair trade products from a tiny niche market to a staple in many stores – and even more households – around the world. At times scoffed at by some as a fad or even a diversion, the concept of fair trade has instead been the source of inspiration to millions, and the leading edge of a sea change in the ways that many consumers relate to people around the world who provide everything from staples like rice and fruits to the luxuries of their day-to-day lives. In the twenty-first century, the expansion and further development of fair trade concepts and products provides all of us with a reminder and a method to live more ethical lives.

Mary Robinson*

---

* Mary Robinson is president of Realizing Rights: The Ethical Globalization Initiative, and former President of Ireland (1990–97) and UN High Commissioner for Human Rights (1997–2002).

The Fairtrade Foundation

The Fairtrade Foundation's vision is of a world in which justice and sustainable development are at the heart of trade structures and practices so that everyone, through their work, can maintain a decent and dignified livelihood and develop their full potential. The Foundation is the independent body in the UK that licences the use of the FAIRTRADE Mark on products certified against internationally agreed standards, set by Fairtrade Labelling Organisations International (FLO). The Foundation also raises public awareness and campaigns for fairer global trade.

Fairtrade provides a better deal for producers in developing countries

Fairtrade standards aim to strengthen the position of small-scale farmers and workers in developing countries. They include an agreed price paid to the farmers' organisations for their crop, helping them meet the costs of production and provide for their families. An additional amount of money, known as a Fairtrade premium, is also paid to farmers' organisations to be spent on community projects of their own choice. Farmers and farm workers decide together how to spend this money, empowering them to create positive change for the future of their own communities.

An estimated 7 million people – farmers, workers and their families – in 60 countries benefit directly from Fairtrade sales, and millions more through the investment of Fairtrade premiums into local business and community improvements.

You can find out more about us at www.fairtrade.org.uk. To find out about Fairtrade around the world go to www.fairtrade.net.

Preface

It is rare in life to have a moment of personal epiphany. Mine came in the millennium year when, at the Co-op, we had just introduced the UK's first own brand Fairtrade product: a chocolate bar with its key ingredient sourced from Ghana. We had supported the concept of fair trade right from the beginning but, although always empathetic to the ethical agenda, my interest was primarily commercial; the intention was to develop responsible retailing, a holistic approach to this agenda, as a modern day reflection of cooperative values and a vehicle for differentiating the business from its competitors. But in concert with the chocolate initiative a BBC crew visited Kuapa Kokoo in Ghana and their 14-minute film changed my view of the world. At the end of their report they unwrapped a chocolate bar, which was starting to melt in the heat, and gave some to a young woman and her daughter. As they tasted the product their eyes lit up and their faces were transformed into bright smiles and the young woman said 'oh, it's so sweet, so sweet'. This lady had spent her whole life toiling in the fields for a pittance and had never tasted the product of her own labours; she had no concept of what it was about chocolate that made it so important and appealing to the people living thousands of miles away in the northern hemisphere. In one sense the film captured a joyous experience but in another it was extraordinarily sad. I felt a catch in my throat and knew I was hooked for the rest of my life.

I spent a great many years at the Co-op and worked with some terrific people who embraced its values and worked hard to further its responsible retailing agenda. These early 'pioneers' included Duncan Bowdler, Peter Jackson, Malcolm Hepworth, Martin Henderson, Wendy Wrigley, Peter Rogan, Bill Shannon and John Chapple. Special mention should also be made of David Croft, Debbie Robinson, Ged Carter, Terry Hudghton, Brad Hill and David Seaman.

This book was first conceived in January 2008 when I was working for AgroFair UK. At that time we were planning the shareholders meeting which was due to take place in the UK the following June. This was when the farmers who are members and shareholders of AgroFair would get together to interrogate our management performance and discuss our strategy for the future. The intention was to use the occasion not just to fulfil the formal shareholders agenda but, as we had farmers together from across the southern hemisphere, to give them the opportunity to see a little of the UK Lake District, visit retail stores, meet a local hill farmer, and socialise with consumers and campaigners in Keswick. We also held a seminar on fair trade at South Africa House where the farmers had the opportunity to put questions to some famous and influential people including Gareth Thomas MP who was then the Minister for International Development. The initial intention had been to publish the papers presented at the seminar, together with some additional contributions from fair trade specialists, as a book to help inform, influence, and inspire people to support fair trade.

Unfortunately time and circumstance scuppered the initial plan, but in 2009, during my second attempt at retirement, I turned my attention once more to this project. The authors are different from those originally planned, and the book is more wide ranging in its scope, but its essential objective remains the same: to promote the concept of fair trade. My gratitude should naturally be extended to all of the contributors to the book but also to the team at AgroFair UK who helped conceive the project. These include Clive Marriott, Paul Harwood, Begona Lozano, Andrea Olivar, Samantha Davis, Lucy Bessant, Margaret Rooke, Robin Murray and Rachel Archer. Extra special thanks should also go to Rachel, for her input into the development of the book over the last two years, and to Lisa Bowes, my daughter, for her English language skills, keen copy eye, and technical wizardry in this computer dependent age. Thanks also to Harriet Lamb and all her colleagues at the Fairtrade Foundation who have given their active and enthusiastic support to this project.

John Bowes

Contributors

Rachel Archer, formerly of AgroFair and Twin, is an experienced traveller who has spent most of the last four years meeting and living with people who work on the land in the global south.

John Bowes was a top manager in the Co-op's retail business and was responsible for the conception and development of the Group's responsible retailing programme. Now retired, his last formal appointment was as managing director of AgroFair UK.

Alex Cole was the Corporate Responsibility director for Cadbury during the formation of the Cadbury Cocoa Partnership and the move to Fairtrade.

David Croft is the global director of Conformance and Sustainability for Cadbury. He was previously a key member of the Co-operative Group's retail team where he helped develop their responsible retailing programme.

Bruce Crowther MBE is the campaigner who established Garstang, Lancashire, as the world's first Fairtrade town.

Pedro Haslam was an opponent of the Somoza dictatorship and has had a long term involvement with fair trade coffee. Elected to the national assembly on the Sandinistas ticket in 2006, he was recently elected as president of Infocoop and appointed as president of the Institute for Rural Development.

Nicholas Hoskyns is a British-born campaigner who went to Nicaragua to support the revolution and has lived and worked there for the past two decades. He is currently managing director of Etico, an ethical trading and investment company which assists small cooperatives in developing sustainable trading initiatives in the global north.

Joe Human MBE is secretary of the Keswick and District Fairtrade campaign and coordinator of the Cumbrian Fairtrade network.

Jeroen Kroezen was one of the founders of El Guabo and managing director of AgroFair Europe. He is currently coordinating the coffee and fruit programmes for Solidaridad in the Netherlands.

Harriet Lamb CBE is executive director of the Fairtrade Foundation.

Tomy Mathew was one of the founders of the Fair Trade Alliance Kerala. He is a director of the Fairtrade Foundation and of Liberation Foods.

Robin Murray was one of the co-founders of Twin where he has been a director for over twenty years, including ten as chairman. Formerly the chairman of both Agrofair UK and Liberation Foods he was identified by *The Guardian* in 2008 as 'one of the fifty people who could save the planet'.

Matt North was the Sainsbury's buyer responsible for masterminding the switch of their banana category to Fairtrade. He is now with A.G. Thames.

Jonathan Rosenthal was the co-founder and former executive director of Equal Exchange, the first fair trade tea and coffee organisation in the US.

1
Introduction
A Brilliant Idea

John Bowes

It is perhaps a little predictable to start a book about fair trade by referring to its dramatic growth over recent years. But the results have been truly impressive. The FAIRTRADE Mark is now almost ubiquitous and recognised by more than 70 per cent of adults in the United Kingdom.[1] And, in a decade, sales of Fairtrade products have increased more than forty-fold to a staggering £800 million in 2009.[2]

This is a spectacular achievement. It is a level of success which few can have anticipated.

Fair trade's remarkable progress reflects the innate decency and instinctive humanitarianism of the UK consumer; the enthusiasm and commitment of thousands of active supporters; the focused and determined leadership of the Fairtrade Foundation; and the visionary, and sometimes courageous, strategic determination of key actors in the UK retail business.

Ordinary people, anxious to make a positive connection with, and in support of, impoverished farmers in the developing world, have embraced the concept of fair trade. The development of the FAIRTRADE Mark, and the determination of the Fairtrade Foundation to keep pace with rapidly accelerating customer demand, has played a critical role in providing consumers with a simple mechanism through which to give a practical manifestation of their desire to support the poor and under-privileged. The Co-op's pioneering role in introducing the FAIRTRADE Mark onto own brand products; Tesco's introduction of a comprehensive own brand range in 2004; and Sainsbury's decision to stock only Fairtrade bananas – all represent seminal moments in establishing momentum for the fair trade revolution.

With all of this activity, and the spin and hype which has surrounded it, a disinterested observer might be excused for concluding that some kind of fundamental and irrevocable change has taken place and that the world trading system was being seriously challenged by a consumer-led revolution. Unfortunately this is still far from being the case.

It has been estimated that fair trade may, currently, be benefiting more than 7 million people in the developing world.[3] This is an impressive achievement but set in the context of the sheer scale of world poverty it still represents only a relatively small contribution towards addressing an enormous problem.

It is estimated that 1.4 billion people, one fifth of the world's population, are trying to survive at or below the World Bank's official poverty line of just $1.25 a day. And 2.6 billion people, about 40 per cent of humanity, are living on less than $2 a day.[4]

These astonishing numbers are so large that it is difficult to fully comprehend them. They reflect the appalling collective failure of human society. And the scale of the failure becomes even more dramatic when we consider *disparities* in world income. The poorest 40 per cent account for just 5 per cent of global income whilst the richest 20 per cent take three quarters of the pot.[5] The truth is that fair trade is still very much in its infancy. Those who are committed to making a real difference in the developing world will recognise that we are not at the end of a process, or anywhere near the end, but really only at the very beginning. If we strip away all of the commercial spin, and occasional wishful thinking, we might be left with the uncomfortable conclusion that, far from capitalising on a consumer movement, we have perhaps not yet recognised its full potential and have so far failed to put mechanisms into place to ensure that its momentum can be fully realised.

There have been a number of surveys on ethical consumers in recent times and what they broadly conclude is that about 5 per cent of UK adults take ethical issues very seriously while around another 20 per cent have an empathy with the ethical agenda.[6] Fair trade has a strong appeal to both of these groups and, therefore, it doesn't take a degree in advanced mathematics to conclude that fair trade ought to appeal to about a quarter of all adults. If we consider that the UK grocery market is estimated to be worth around £140 billion it is clear that sales of Fairtrade products still have a long way to go. With annual sales of £800 million they still account for less than 1 per cent of total grocery sales.

The concept of fair trade has been around since the 1960s when growing concern about neo-imperialism, the growth of multinational corporations, and the plight of producers in the developing world gave birth to the concept of 'Trade not Aid'. In 1965 Oxfam launched 'Helping-by-Selling' – a programme which sold imported handicrafts, from cooperatives and community enterprises in the developing world, through its mail order catalogue and its high street stores. In 1969 the first

Worldshop, a business dedicated to selling handicrafts produced under fair conditions, was launched in the Netherlands; it was successful and further shops were subsequently introduced in other Western European countries. In 1985 Twin (Third World Information Network) was founded with the support of the Greater London Council; politically subversive in its early days it initiated its distinguished record as a fair trade pioneer by importing cigars from Cuba and rocking chairs from Nicaragua.

The initial development of fair trade products was not based on any conception of mainstream market potential but on the genuine concerns of a relatively small number of activists about poverty-stricken farmers in the global south. These pioneers sought to establish new trading models whereby producers achieved improved market access and received a fairer reward for their products. However, with the marketing focused on alternative trading organisations, sales were dependent upon a narrow but committed activist base. As important and well-intentioned as these people were, a fundamental sea change was required if these products were ever going to have a material impact in the marketplace.

In 1988 Solidaridad, a Dutch Christian development agency, established Max Havelaar, the first fair trade label, and began selling fair trade coffee to Dutch supermarkets.[7] The initiative offered disadvantaged producers a fair price for their crop and independent certification allowed the goods to be sold into the mainstream for the very first time. This was a brilliant idea and a groundbreaking innovation. Within a few years it had been replicated across Europe and North America and its success led to the establishment of the Fairtrade Labelling Organizations International (FLO) in 1997. Based in Germany, its primary task has been to bring all of these national initiatives together behind universal fair trade standards and a single mark.

The development of the FAIRTRADE Mark not only offered the customer a simple shorthand, implicitly communicating proof of audit and accreditation, it also opened up major new distribution opportunities by providing retailers with a credible and recognisable vehicle through which to focus and deliver on their own ethical credentials. In addition, its resultant ubiquity has helped to reinforce the fair trade message and the universal recognition of the central issues involved.

The FAIRTRADE Mark represents a visual guarantee that a product has met international Fairtrade standards. These include a guaranteed minimum price set at a level which ensures that the producer is able to cover all costs necessary for sustainable production. This is not a fixed price. If the market price for a product increases beyond the Fairtrade minimum then the producer will receive the higher of the two prices. The minimum price is set by FLO and ensures that, even when world prices fall, the farmer always receives enough money to cover costs and stay in business.

The mark also guarantees the Fairtrade premium. This is a sum of money, in addition to the product price, which is paid for investment in social, environmental or development projects. The premium is fixed by FLO and its use is determined demo-cratically by producers and/or workers within the farming business. It might, for instance, be invested in healthcare, education, or be used to support commercial projects which support the sustained viability of the farming enterprise.

The standards also recognise that importers in the north will, under usual circumstances, have much better access to credit than producers in developing countries. Accordingly, importers are required to be prepared to pre-finance up to 60 per cent of the purchase value of seasonal crops. This can sometimes be critical for producer cooperatives as they often need to pay their members at time of delivery in order to compete with private traders.

The Fairtrade standards also emphasise the importance of partnership between trading partners. Long term trading relationships allow producers to plan with the confidence that they have a secure market for their products. This allows them to build capacity, invest in technology and strengthen their organisations. Indeed, there is substantial evidence to suggest that sustainable market access is as important as Fairtrade premium prices for many marginal producers in the developing world.[8]

Producers also have to demonstrate that they are adhering to specific economic, environmental and social requirements. The initial standards were established with the intention of establishing criteria for small-scale farmers and, therefore, focused on cooperatives or similar associations. These organisations are required to have a democratic structure and a transparent administration; facilitating effective control of the management by empowering their members. Discrimination on the basis of race, colour, sex, religion, political opinion, national extraction or social origin is strictly outlawed.

Separate standards have been established to apply to companies who employ hired labour. Where workers are employed they must have the right to freedom of association and collective bargaining, be free from any form of discrimination, have fair conditions of employment, and operate in a safe working environment. Children under 15 cannot be contracted for employment.

Producers' organisations must ensure that their members limit their impact on the natural environment by making environmental protection an integral part of farm management. New planting in virgin forest areas is strictly prohibited. Organic production is encouraged but, where this is not socially and economically practical, the use of pesticides has to be minimised. FLO publishes a list of agrochemicals which are strictly prohibited. The use of genetically modified organisms are also banned.

Clearly, these standards have important implications for both producers and traders; both have obligations to fulfil if the integrity of the FAIRTRADE Mark is to be protected. In order to ensure that these obligations are being met, a comprehensive auditing process has been put into place.

FLO-Cert is an international certification company which is owned by Fairtrade Labelling Organizations International but which is effectively autonomous and operates independently. All processors and exporters in the producer countries must have their products certified by FLO-Cert. The process is simple. Producers who apply for certification are visited by an inspector who assesses their level of compliance with Fairtrade standards. The inspector's report is then considered by the FLO-Cert certification committee which will only issue a certificate if the required standards have been met. Producers already in the system are re-inspected on an annual basis in order to ensure that the standards are being maintained.

The products of importers and companies outside of the producer country are certified by either FLO-Cert or by the local labelling authority. The Fairtrade Foundation is responsible for certifying products entering the UK. It is their role to provide an independent certification of the trade chain. In effect, they license the FAIRTRADE Mark to companies for use on products which comply with Fairtrade standards. They set up a licensing agreement with each company specifying the products which may carry the mark, approve every separate use of the mark, and audit each licensed company's Fairtrade activities.

The Fairtrade Foundation's mission is to work with businesses, community groups and individuals to improve the position of producers in the south. One of their key activities has been to raise public awareness of the need for fair trade and the importance of the FAIRTRADE Mark. In this, they have been remarkably successful.

They have tapped the potential of the activist movement by encouraging local campaigns in support of fair trade, most notably through the concept of Fairtrade towns. This idea first drew breath in the small town of Garstang when, in 2001, a small group of activists persuaded local businesses, and the local authority, to make an active and positive commitment to fair trade. There are now 400 Fairtrade towns, 1,500 Fairtrade schools and 4,000 faiths groups, all actively supporting fair trade within their communities. These initiatives had the dual impact of raising an awareness of the fair trade concept and, initially, helping to create a small but growing market for Fairtrade products.

However, the Foundation's most important contribution has resulted from the effective way it has leveraged the potential of the FAIRTRADE Mark. Whilst the early marketing of fair trade products focused on alternative trading organisations like Oxfam, the development of the FAIRTRADE Mark opened up dramatic new opportunities for these products. The 1990s witnessed the development of a number of specialist businesses, committed to fair trade, which, together, represented a sea change in the marketing of fair trade products. They recognised the need to improve the public's perception of the quality of fair trade products. Whatever the intrinsic quality of the basic raw materials some of the earliest products were not well profiled for European tastes and for some the initial product experience created a lingering prejudice. Low levels of customer satisfaction were bound to inhibit market penetration. If fair trade was to break into the mainstream it had to reposition its product offer on a much stronger quality platform. The respective introductions of Cafédirect, Divine chocolate and OKE bananas represented pivotal moments in a shift towards the mainstream. The development of specialist brands was a determined attempt to reach an emerging ethical market via the shelves of high street retailers.

But the introduction of the FAIRTRADE Mark also paved the way for own brand development and with this fair trade was well set on the growth pattern with which we are now so familiar. The Co-op led the way when it introduced the first Fairtrade own brand product in the millennium year; a milk chocolate bar, marketed in conjunction with the Day (Divine) Chocolate Company, and carefully profiled to match UK tastes.

While the Co-op was the early pioneer, real volume progress could not be made without engaging the big four multiple retailers – Tesco, Asda, Sainsbury's and Morrisons – who dominate UK food retailing and together account for about 75 per cent of the grocery market. All four of these retailers put an early toe in the market but the real breakthrough came in 2004 when Tesco, by far the largest UK retailer, introduced a comprehensive range of Fairtrade products.[9] And it was the multiple retail trade which has subsequently driven the growth of fair trade in the UK. They have provided critical access to millions of customers and been proactive in developing new Fairtrade products. What started as a small business based on the sale of a few handicrafts, and a little bit of coffee, now encompasses a great many different products including bananas, pineapples, melons, mangoes, grapefruit, chocolate, tea, cotton, honey, juices, nuts, rice, wine, flowers, and footballs.

But for some these changes presented a dilemma. Many activists and campaigners were concerned that this leap from a limited but ethically holistic supply chain into a volume mainstream market, through the vehicle of large multiple retailers, represented a challenge. For some it was tantamount to sleeping with the enemy and it presented a difficult choice. They could stand firm against the tide but, in doing so, recognise that their own moral and ethical integrity was being purchased at the expense of many poor people in the developing world; or they could embrace change and accept that, whilst their personal principles might be compromised, the benefits of fair trade would reach a great deal further; literally millions of desperate people might benefit.

An almost immediate impact of the move into the mainstream was the requirement for Fairtrade Labelling Organizations International to set up hired labour standards. The volume demands of the big retailers necessitated bringing large plantations into the fair trade system. For many activists this was an issue of serious concern. For them fair trade was not just about paying a bit more for the products but also about working with cooperatives to support livelihoods, sustain families, their communities and way of life; and to help create strong, sustainable and democratically organised working environments in the countryside. The legitimisation of large plantations not only undermined this concept but also established a real potential threat to the smallholders they had initially set out to support; how could small democratically organised cooperatives compete effectively with large well-managed privately owned farming businesses?

The dilemma of the mainstream was brought into the sharpest possible focus when Nestlé, the *bête noire* of the ethical movement, communicated their intention to introduce a single variety of their extensive coffee range as a Fairtrade product. Nestlé have been the target of a boycott in many countries because, it is alleged, that they have aggressively marketed baby foods in the developing world, in contravention of World Health Organization marketing requirements, and, as a consequence, have contributed to the suffering of millions of infants. They are also one of the world's top five coffee roasters who, between them, had been on the receiving end of a campaign attacking their role in pushing down prices so low that many small farmers had endured terrible suffering.[10]

Hence the dilemma when Nestlé introduced its Partners' Blend. If this represented a fundamental change of position by one of the world's top coffee roasters then it potentially represented an enormous breakthrough. Millions of people might ultimately benefit. On the other hand, if it simply represented a cynical and opportunist exploitation of the potential in the emerging ethical market then it might undermine the integrity and sustainability of the whole project.[11]

Whatever Nestlé's motivation and intentions they cannot be singled out for accusations of opportunism. As fair trade has moved into the mainstream it has inevitably involved businesses in the distributive industries that have been drawn in by its commercial potential rather than by any commitment to its social and trading goals. On the positive side this has enabled fair trade to grow rapidly. On the negative side, it is obvious that many of these businesses would just as rapidly switch out from fair trade in a downturn as they have switched into it during its growth cycle. They are simply partners of convenience.

What is for sure is that businesses which have no real commitment to fair trade, and have been drawn to it reluctantly, in response to changing customer expectations, are not only the ones most likely to ditch it if times change, they are also the least likely to carry the agenda forward as the fair trade movement seeks to raise standards and pass on a greater share of the supply chain benefits to people in the developing world. The opportunists are the prophets of the lowest common denominator. They exist to serve the needs of their shareholders and not to inspire any fundamental change in global trading practices. Their inclination will always be to commit to the least they believe they can credibly get away with whilst staying within the strict letter of the rules. Certainly, there is no prospect of these businesses pushing the agenda along and extending the scope and scale of the benefits flowing into the south.

There is no doubt that the simple mechanism of the Fairtrade price has brought great benefits to millions of poor people but anyone who has visited Fairtrade Farms in Africa, Asia, Central and South America, or the Caribbean will recognise that, great as it is, it hardly delivers European-style comforts. The farmers and workers still have a pretty tough existence. One of the key forward challenges for the fair trade movement is how to generate a greater level of wealth transference; finding the means to ensure that more money is retained by, or returned to, the people who need it the most.

Customer expectations are changing all of the time. And the issue of climate change has, after a long gestation period, shot right to the top of the agenda. Millions have now seen former US Vice President Al Gore's film *An Inconvenient Truth*, high profile political events like the United Nations climate change conference in Copenhagen have dominated the news screen, politicians of virtually every persuasion have openly recognised and espoused climate change as the most important issue of our times, and a series of unusual weather events has brought the issue of global warming right to our very doorsteps. Some or all of these factors have impacted on our awareness. Something has broken through the complacency and finally made people realise that something is not quite right; that something has to be done.

This has important implications for fair trade. The very nature of the whole project involves shipping or flying commodities over enormous distances and, in the process, burning carbon and contributing to global warming. There is no escaping this. There is a trade-off between the benefits that fair trade can bring to the south and the damage which international trade, by its very nature, inflicts on the environment. And from a southern perspective the impact of climate change may run much closer to home. Cafédirect has recently published some work which concludes that rising temperatures and changing patterns of precipitation may already be having dire consequences for coffee farmers.[12] Water shortages, deforestation, degradation of land from salination and pollution, using agricultural land for non-agricultural purposes (biofuels) – all of these issues present serious current and future challenges. From an ethical perspective the far from easy task is to try and find the right formula with which to balance these issues in order to secure the optimum outcome.

As the environment has become such a huge front-of-mind issue it has perhaps assisted the growth of alternative trading marks. The Rainforest Alliance is an international conservation organisation, based in New York, which sets out to conserve biodiversity and ensure sustainable livelihoods. For growers to be certified by the Alliance they must adhere to sustainable agricultural principles that include preserving local wildlife, protecting forests, minimising soil erosion and treating farm workers fairly. The primary emphasis has been on protecting the local environment whilst giving the growers the opportunity of a better life through entry into premium coffee trading. While there are undoubtedly benefits to this approach, the Alliance does not offer producers a minimum or a guaranteed price. This makes it a cheaper way for large brands to tap into the ethical market, effectively allowing them to display an ethical label without having to make any really serious pecuniary investment in wealth transference. A number of large brands, including Kenco and PG Tips, have taken this route into the ethical market as an alternative to embracing the fair trade principles and securing the FAIRTRADE Mark.

The very rapid growth of fair trade has also created its own specific tensions. Large modern retailers, with strong own brand ranges, expect to move quickly from initial product concept through to on-shelf delivery. In contrast, the Fairtrade system, with its inevitably bureaucratic process of certification, has sometimes found it difficult to keep pace. Similarly, really big decisions, like Sainsbury's electing to convert all of their bananas to Fairtrade, can impact on the whole market; for a while, at least, there may not, in some circumstances, be enough accredited product available to meet the anticipated level of demand. Some retailers might grasp the wealth transference mechanics of fair trade more easily than the producers requirement for a stable and sustainable route to market; the danger being that Fairtrade products become commoditised, with the label being more important than the product or its source; and, as a result, some importers might switch their sourcing with little or no regard to the implications for the grower; in effect, the very antithesis of fair trade.[13] These are serious issues. The unenviable task for the Fairtrade Foundation, and their international partners, is to deliver increased scale without compromising on the established standards; to create an efficient and effective environment which connects producers and consumers.

Sales of fair trade products in the United States of America have grown rapidly.[14] In terms of retail value it remains the biggest market in the world for fair trade products; in 2007 the retail value of sales was estimated at €730,000. However, in per capita terms it falls well short of the United Kingdom which has a very much smaller number of inhabitants but sells almost as much fair trade product (€704,000).[15] It has been argued that the relative weakness of fair trade in the United States reflects its culture of self-centred political and emotional isolationism, together with a virtually undeviating commitment to the capitalist market economy, which has, historically, driven the single-minded pursuit of personal material wealth at the expense of an empathetically motivated response to global economic and social problems.[16] If this is true then it represents a major obstacle for fair trade in the future. Success in the largest consumer market on Earth has to be a prerequisite for any fundamental and sustained change in global trading practices. Fair trade has come a long way in a relatively short period. But its progress is still embryonic. It still has an awful long way to go. But of all of the challenges it faces going forward, the United States is perhaps the toughest nut to crack.

With so much of the world's wealth concentrated in the northern hemisphere it follows that fundamental change can only be achieved with the support of consumers in Europe and North America. It is too easy, therefore, to see the success of fair trade as a northern movement; dependent solely on the goodwill and guile of well-intentioned activists and supporters in the United States and Western Europe. Much of what has been achieved so far has also been dependent on some visionary leadership of producer cooperatives in the south. The producer founders of fair trade were not sat around waiting for some enlightened foreign assistance to help address their self-evident problems but were active in seeking out like-minded people who supported their vision of the future. They wanted to see greater equality in the trading system, democratic participation at grassroots level and, proactively through their cooperatives, to improve their position in the supply chain in order to have greater control over their own lives. Many of these southern activists have become key people in the fair trade movement; actively involved on the boards of companies like Cafédirect, AgroFair, Divine and Liberation, as well as Fairtrade Labelling Organizations International and the Fairtrade Foundation. Through their participation in these businesses and organisations they have a key role in shaping the future of fair trade and, by so doing, determine whether it will succeed in evolving from an important but small part role to a full-scale trading revolution.

NOTES

1. The term 'fair trade' is used to refer to the concept of fair trade and the wider movement of producers, businesses and campaigners who support it, and conduct their campaigns and businesses according to its principles. The term 'Fairtrade' is used to describe the international system, standards, certification and products certified by the Fairtrade Labelling Organizations International (FLO). The FAIRTRADE Mark is the registered trademark and format name for the certified mark.

2. 'Sales of Fairtrade Certified Products in the UK', Fairtrade Foundation, www.fairtrade.org.uk

3. See Chapter 2.

4. *World Bank Development Indicators 2008.*

5. *2007 Human Development Report*, United Nations Development Program.

6. Roger Cowe and Simon Williams, *Who are the Ethical Consumers?* Co-operative Bank/MORI, 2000, pp. 26–34.

7. The name emanated from a nineteenth century Dutch novel in which Max Havelaar, the fictional hero, gives up his career to work in solidarity with Indonesian workers.

8. Sally Smith, *For Love or Money? Fairtrade Business Models in the UK Supermarket Sector*, 3rd Fair Trade International Symposium, 14–16 May 2008, Montpellier, France, pp. 7–9.

9. John Bowes and David Croft, 'Organic and Fair Trade Crossover and Convergence', in Simon Wright and Diane McCrea (eds), *The Handbook of Organic and Fair Trade Marketing,* Blackwell, 2007, pp. 267–71.

10. *Mugged: Poverty in Your Coffee Cup*, Oxfam GB, 2002, www.oxfam.org.uk

11. Bowes and Croft, 'Organic and Fair Trade Crossover and Convergence', pp. 272–4.

12. Cafédirect, AdaptCC, www.cafedirect.co.uk

13. Smith, *For Love or Money?* p. 9.

14. Laura T. Raynolds, 'Broadening the Movement and Market in the United States', in Laura T. Raynolds, Douglas Murray and

John Wilkinson (eds), *Fair Trade: The Challenges of Transforming Globilization*, Routledge, 2007, p. 63.

15. 'Estimated Retail Value of Fairtrade Certified Products by Country (in Euros)', Fairtrade Foundation, www.fairtrade.org.uk

16. Bowes and Croft, 'Organic and Fair Trade Crossover and Convergence', p. 279.

Plate 1
Maria and her mangoes, Peru
Courtesy of AgroFair, Rachel Archer

Plate 2
Juan Ramon amongst bean plants on his banana farm,
Dominican Republic

Courtesy of AgroFair, Rachel Archer

Plate 3
Soil teeming with worms on Juan Ramon's banana farm, Dominican Republic
Courtesy of AgroFair, Rachel Archer

Plate 4
Angel Iniguez scouting for shrimps and fish in the fresh water,
unpolluted stream on his banana farm, Ecuador

Courtesy of AgroFair, Rachel Archer

Plate 5
Flowers flourish beneath banana plants on
Angel Iniguez's organic Fairtrade banana farm, Ecuador

Courtesy of AgroFair, Rachel Archer

Plate 6
Oliver Kishero interviewing fellow coffee farmer
Dision Kisombo, Uganda

Courtesy of Gumutindo Coffee Co-operative, Rachel Archer

Plate 7
Rachel Archer learning to prepare plantain staple matoke
with Oliver Kishero and daughter Marian, Uganda

Rachel Archer

Plate 8
Lucia in her kitchen, Nicaragua
Rachel Archer

Plate 9
Some members of the women's co-operative 'New Dawn', Nicaragua
Rachel Archer

Plate 10
Nick Hoskyns, Julio Obregon and Uriel Chavarria in the Cecocafen cupping lab, Nicaragua
Nestor Saavedra Rodriguez

Plate 11
Rolando Lopez Calderon and Luis del Carmen Tercero Rodriguez
from the co-operative Juan Francisco Paz Silva in Achuapa,
Nicaragua, ploughing their land to plant sesame

Katharine Hoskyns

Plate 12
Splitting cocoa pods on a typical Ghanaian farm
Courtesy of Cadbury, David Croft

Plate 13
Anthony Blay (VREL, Ghana), Pedro Miguel Checa Farfan (Apromalpi, Peru),
Jovanny Coronel (El Guabo, Ecuador), Brad Hill (Co-op),
Roberto Ugalde (Asproagroin, Costa Rica), and John Bowes
celebrating the introduction of Fairtrade ice lollies at Maryport Cumbria, 2008

Courtesy of AgroFair, copyright Bethany Murray

Plate 14
Tea picker at Satemwa, Malawi
Copyright Anette Kay

Plate 15
Cashew tree
Courtesy of Equal Exchange

Plate 16
The water supply for a small community in Panama
Courtesy of AgroFair, Clive Marriott

Part I
Producers

2
The Impact of Fairtrade

Harriet Lamb

Rwanda's red rolling hills are covered with millions of subdivided plots sprouting bright green crops. At the airport, a fellow passenger scrabbles around to hide a plastic bag – they are banned here. As he chats to his colleagues, I discover they are arriving for the celebrated Cup of Excellence Awards for top quality coffee. Ten years ago, as Rwanda emerged blinking from its vicious civil war, its coffee was off the map. Today, it's scooping up awards. And coffee matters – to people and the whole country – making up 30 per cent of export earnings.

Before going, I watched the film *Hotel Rwanda*. My daughter kept checking: was I crying, or hiding from the horrors of man's inhumanity to man during the 1994 genocide? Instead, she was amazed by my soppy smile. For no-one can fail to be humbled and inspired by the true story of how hotel manager Paul Rusesabagina saved over 1,000 refugees from the murdering mobs, showing endless ingenuity and a deep well of humanity. That really is having the courage of your convictions.

Today, it is equally hard not to be humbled and inspired by how Rwandans – from senior civil servants to coffee farmers

– are pulling together with remarkable focus and ingenuity, to tackle the poverty that blights lives and can feed conflicts, to regenerate their economy and rebuild society.

I visited Maraba village, where a bustling market, busy bank and a choice of hairdressing 'saloons' are all lively testimony to the economic revival stimulated by the villagers' coffee cooperative. Ten years ago, this village was recorded as among the country's poorest with people literally dying of hunger; their aptly named 'café ordinaire' fetching less than ordinary prices. Today, the Maraba villagers are commanding handsome premiums and winning prizes for their speciality coffee. Ten years ago, Angelique's family sold raw coffee berries to passing middlemen; today, in a white coat, she is the first generation of cuppers in the cooperative's own laboratory, skilled in the techniques used to evaluate the aroma and flavour of coffee, feeding back to the farmers, improving quality. Today, they roast and sell their own coffee locally in Rwanda, and export to, among others, Union Hand Roasted who sell Rwanda Maraba Fairtrade coffee in the UK.

Visiting the Maraba farmers with me was Mark Price, the bubbly boss of Waitrose, nicknamed the 'chubby grocer'. He was moved and impressed, saying: 'Visiting growers in Rwanda reinforced my view that through Fairtrade, there is a more morally just way of sourcing from developing countries. I was struck by the Maraba cooperative's pride in producing excellent quality coffee – so the Fairtrade premiums can drive a virtuous circle. Fairtrade is now a proven model to raise the most disadvantaged out of poverty and I hope that one day all developing world commodities will be traded in this way.'

Fair trade is above all else a worldwide people's movement to create that fairer trading system. At its beating heart are farmers and workers who, maybe for the first time in their lives, can sell their crops with a sense of fairness and empowerment; and shoppers here who can give thought to those who grew the cocoa in their chocolate bar or the beans in their morning coffee.

As more and more people are choosing Fairtrade, more doors have opened to more producers. By 2010, 879 producer organisations in 58 developing countries were participating in Fairtrade. Over 460 groups were selling to the UK alone. Even as I type, these numbers are rising: the first standards have just been announced, for example, for Fairtrade and Fairmined certified gold, opening windows to artisanal miners for the very first time and letting the winds of change blow through that industry.

As Fairtrade expands, so the reading pile of academic studies sitting on my desk grows ever higher. These weighty papers are full of the objective evidence and analysis we need constantly to identify how to improve the system, and to get an overarching sense of the difference Fairtrade is making across the producing communities. There are studies underway with banana producers in the Dominican Republic, Ecuador, the Windward Islands and Ghana through to sugar, tea and peanut producer groups in Malawi. Like the individual stories, so the studies all sing stories of change – for couples, for communities, even sometimes for countries. The nature of that change varies from group to group. What they have in common is that Fairtrade has supported them to develop their democracy, transparency, participation and empowerment as well as having an economic impact.

But the constant refrain is also – way to go, guys, way to go. Because in the race to change world trade, we are hardly out of the starting blocks. And our system needs constant pit-stops to fix, adapt – and to grow.

The icing on that analytical cake will always be the individuals whose stories touch your soul and run electric through the impact. Gerardo Arias Camacho tips back his ever-present coffee as he captivates staff at BT's London headquarters who have just switched their hot beverages to Fairtrade, following a campaign led by the Connect trade union. As eloquently charming as he is personally passionate, he sketches out what Fairtrade means to an individual, to him. Born on a small coffee farm in Costa Rica, he had to leave school after four short years when coffee prices plummeted in 1980: 'I did miss school a lot. I really wanted to keep studying. I cried every day probably for around a year because it's not easy being 10 years old and having to work on the coffee farm.'

At 18, with the farm still struggling to provide for the family, he determined to chance his luck emigrating illegally into the US: 'I dreamt of buying a small pick-up truck to carry the coffee to the mill and also to take my mother to doctor's appointments.' A country boy, he was 'as scared as a chicken in a wolf's lair… it was a nightmare'.

At every stage, crooks ripped him off, stealing his scrimped savings with plastic promises. For six days – including three walking across the US border desert – he had no food or drink apart from the hand basin on a coach that he kept drinking dry! Years of hardship followed until he saved enough to go home. That's why he literally shakes with anger when he hears theoretical economists pontificate that farmers should diversify out of coffee. Into precisely what livelihood, he asks? And that's why he determined that his kids should not have to leave their village. So he went back to Costa Rica to help lead a Fairtrade coffee cooperative, Coocafe, that enables farmers to stay on their land, and that educates their kids:

It helps the poorest families to send their children to school so they won't have the same problems I had. In my co-op we have 26 students in high school and nine at university. So these kids will have a better future and will be able to get good jobs and won't have to emigrate like I did. We also get more money directly in our pockets from the coffee we sell through Fairtrade terms which allows us to stay on our farms and to get enough money to cover our expenses and keep our families.

Listening to Gerardo in full flow, I'm reminded that behind him stand an astounding seven and a half million farmers, workers and their dependants whose lives have been lifted through Fairtrade. Not magically transformed into a bed of roses for they are still wrestling with so very many problems. But maybe given a new outlook, given that architecture of hope.

The largest number of Fairtrade groups is still concentrated in Latin America, where Fairtrade labelling was first conceived, rising phoenix-like from the bitter ashes of the collapse of coffee prices in the late 1980s. To the outsider, some countries in this continent such as Mexico or Costa Rica may seem relatively better-off but too often smallholders are among their poorest citizens. For many, Fairtrade has been a lifeline.

Over the five years to 2010, the Fairtrade Foundation has teamed up with the Africa Fairtrade Network of producer groups to change this geographic picture. In Africa, the number of Fairtrade certified organisations rose from 42 in 12 countries in 2002, to 214 organisations from 26 countries going into 2009. Focus breeds interest; interest breeds action.

The chances for different producers to access the Fairtrade system have widened considerably. In the early days, coffee was king. Soon producers were queuing up, insisting that Fairtrade should apply to their products too. Now, producers of wine grapes to flowers, dried and fresh fruit, nuts, cotton, olive oil and far more besides, are able to access Fairtrade markets.

Around 100 new groups enter the Fairtrade system annually. That's thanks to pretty steep growth. But it's not enough. Producers are knocking on our doors, wanting to enter the system or to sell more of their crop.

Independent research has indicated that Fairtrade's direct and indirect impacts run in four ways.

1. FINANCIAL BENEFITS

These come from the Fairtrade minimum price, the additional Fairtrade premium, the pre-financing often made available to producer groups to enable farmers to purchase seed, for example, and the longer term trading relationships which bring additional security. The research group the Natural Resources Institute chewed their way through an astonishing 33 studies[1] of Fairtrade and found that in 31, the producers gained positive economic benefits. Families often enjoy higher returns and more stable incomes than farmers selling to the conventional market.

Fairtrade Labelling Organizations International (FLO), the global Fairtrade coordinator, estimates that, in 2009, producers earned an extra €52 million in Fairtrade premiums. Of course, often it's the minimum price that is more significant but that's much tougher to calculate because conventional prices fluctuate so wildly. An early study in Uganda and Tanzania found that it was only because of the higher Fairtrade price and Fairtrade premium that some coffee cooperatives were able to survive the devastating collapse in market prices in 2001.

In many cases, the fact that some groups are selling on Fairtrade terms can even raise prices for neighbouring non-Fairtrade groups. Coffee groups in Bolivia found that Fairtrade became a price-setter with a number of groups close to them also able to negotiate higher prices for their crops. In Malawi, Dyborn Chibonga is the very tall and elegant leader of the National Smallholder Farmers' Association of Malawi (NASFAM) who is also, I discover on his trip to London, a fan of *The Sound of Music*! He told me how in its first years with Fairtrade, NASFAM took on a 'price-setting' role: once it announces the price it will pay for the annual crop of peanuts, other traders match this price in order to attract quality nuts. Producer groups in Tanzania, Peru, Ghana, Nicaragua and India among others have similarly reported that other buyers have upped their prices because of the competition induced by Fairtrade.

Likewise, researchers in Ghana found that improvements in labour conditions first implemented on the Fairtrade certified plantation, spread to other plantations in the region.

Farmers also often report that the impact of Fairtrade ripples wider in the local economy. For example, where farmers and workers have more in their pockets, they spend more. So others open village shops – some selling groceries, others farm goods – which also saves the whole community long treks to buy their basics.

Another common benefit is that Fairtrade gives farmers the security, the capital and the knowledge to diversify their source of income, reducing their dangerous dependence on one crop. Many farmers are able to invest in small livestock production. In some cases, the women have used the capital to set up handicraft businesses, vegetable plots, bakeries and other small businesses. The Kilimanjaro Native Cooperative Union (KNCU) in Tanzania have invested additional income from Fairtrade into a community Tourist programme, called Kahawa Shamba, which provides an alternative income stream to coffee farming families in the area.

The credit crunch is now on everyone's lips. But for smallholders and workers, credit has always been top of their problem list – and the banks' doors remain shut in their faces. When I visited tea estates in South India, workers told me how on pay day, the moneylenders start rolling into the village in their flash new 4 x 4s to collect repayments at extortionate rates. Which explains why so many academic studies found that access to credit is a particular benefit of Fairtrade, either through pre-financing by buyers, credit schemes set up by the farmers and workers using the premium, or because organised groups with their longer term Fairtrade contracts are considered a better 'risk' and can get into the bank.

2. ACCESS TO MARKETS

Some producer groups have only ever sold their crop locally until they enter Fairtrade. For them, Fairtrade's greatest impact is the doors it opens to better paying overseas markets, often accompanied by technical and organisational support provided by companies. The success of the Heiveld Rooibos Tea Cooperative in South Africa, for example, is put down to the access to a high value market through Fairtrade; supportive relationships with a network of buyers including from dedicated company Equal Exchange; plus direct assistance for infrastructure, business development and training from the Environmental Monitoring Group (EMG), a local NGO. Benefits to the local community include a greater sense of community as well as increased incomes and more jobs.

3. EMPOWERMENT

Time and again, farmers say that, despite all the tangible benefits of Fairtrade, the greatest impact is hardest to describe. Empowerment is an ugly, clunky word but no-one has found another way to encapsulate how farmers can change their position in the supply chain, and the chance Fairtrade can give workers to organise into trades unions to represent their interests.

John Kanjagaile is the beaming, jovial Export Manager of the KCU cooperative of coffee smallholders in the dry North West of Tanzania. He tells me how the farmers used to sell their beans to the first middleman who came along with no idea of where they went. Now the farmers are well organised, exporting their coffee directly themselves and are part-owners of a local instant coffee processing factory and brand, as well as of leading Fairtrade company Cafédirect. Now when John passes through the village, the farmers call out to him: 'Hey John. What's the price on the New York coffee exchange today?' Because now the farmers know where their coffee goes and how the market works.

In fact, one group of authors argue that increasing the strength of producer groups and their bargaining power is the single most important impact of Fairtrade – beyond the actual value of the products traded.

4. NETWORKING OPPORTUNITIES

Smallholders also benefit from participating in associations such as the Committee of Latin American and Caribbean producers (CLAC) or Fairtrade Africa. These networks part-own Fairtrade Labelling Organizations International, and give producers the opportunity to collaborate and discuss issues in an organised forum. They can exchange ideas, mull over shared problems and feed into global policies.

Some producers also part-own dedicated companies such as Cafédirect, Divine Chocolate, fresh fruit pioneers AgroFair and the newcomer, nut company Liberation, giving the producers a say in how their crops are sold and marketed right the way to the supermarket shelf, as well as a share in the profits.

If Fairtrade's impact arises mainly through these four mechanisms, it is lived out in several different ways:

IMPACT FOR PRODUCERS AND THEIR FAMILIES

Gerardo Arias Camacho explains how, for members of Coocafe, 'the Fairtrade price allows us to survive as coffee farmers. It covers our costs of production, lets us send our kids to school, buy clothes and keep a roof over our heads.' Also in Costa Rica, the farmers of Asoproagroìn, produced the world's first Fairtrade pineapples and told the same story – that Fairtrade was enabling families to stay together, allowing farmers to remain on their land when options are limited rather than risking all by travelling to the cities to look for work – with destitution too often the result.

It is a story that plays a constant beat among all the farmers I have met: that Fairtrade is helping farmers stay on their land and meet their basic needs while providing education and new opportunities for their children. Furthermore, the empowerment at the heart of the Fairtrade system benefits individual workers and farmers who, studies report, have improved self-confidence and self-esteem as well as access to training or education. At Satemwa Tea Estates in Malawi, training and support has been provided through Fairtrade for financial management, bookkeeping and budgeting. In fact, Satemwa now runs the largest adult education programme in the whole country.

IMPACT ON PRODUCER ORGANISATIONS

The reputation of Ugandan coffee slipped down following liberalisation of the industry. The Gumutindo Cooperative, supported by Fairtrade and in particular its relationship with Cafédirect, has invested in agricultural training, organic conversion and improved processing methods to raise the quality of its coffee. Buyers are now knocking on the cooperative's door and farmers are queuing up to join the organisation.

This organisational strengthening is a magic key, unlocking long term sustainable change. As one study states:

The success in self-organisation seems to be far more important (than just price), resulting in better bargaining positions, better credit worthiness and economies of scale. The fair-trade system contributes to these organisational successes through capacity building, an initial guaranteed market, linkages with the international market and learning-by-doing in exporting. In addition, and similarly to the organic cases, Fair-trade contributed to quality improvements.[2]

As farmers become organised and empowered, they can step slowly, rung by rung, up a ladder of change. Some now export direct themselves; or process their crop; or even own the final brand – as with Kuapa Kokoo and Divine Chocolate; and the brazil nut, cashew and peanut farming groups from eight countries who co-own Liberation.

IMPACT ON THE COMMUNITY

In Mali, only four out of ten children are in school – because there are so few schools, some have to walk ten miles. So not surprisingly, women cotton farmers in the Dougourakoroni cooperative decided to spend their first Fairtrade premium payment on building a small two-room schoolhouse. But it was overflowing as children crowded into the tiny rooms. So the next year when they earned their premium, the members, now feeling empowered, negotiated with the local government to ensure that they too lived up to their responsibilities. The result – the village now also has a smarter three-room school building with some 160 pupils funded jointly by the local government and the cooperative.

The wider community of course benefits from the success of local cooperatives. But they also directly benefit from the myriad of programmes that producers have undertaken using the Fairtrade premium – buying computers, sterilising equipment or ambulances, bringing electricity and clean water to villages for the first time, building clinics and schools and roads, investing in the environment... it is a proud roll call.

A study of the Ghanaian cocoa-producing group, Kuapa Kokoo, found that the community projects funded through the Fairtrade premium were having a development impact upon the wider community as well as Kuapa members.[3] For example, more than 100,000 people in the community benefited from free medical attention and prescriptions, and a school building project funded by the premium had 'emphatically improved pupil attendance and health and the quality of education'.

Debates are often heated over how to choose between strong competing needs. In Malawi, the NASFAM peanut farmers decided to use their first premium payment to build a shelter for carers at the District hospital precisely because this would benefit the greatest number of people from the widest area. Until then, families caring for patients just lived outside under the trees. Now the farmers are weighing up the next priorities. It is no easy task and the farmers' plans are often constrained by the amount they can sell on Fairtrade terms.

The tiny Windward Islands in the Caribbean offer a little window of insight into just how far-reaching the impact of Fairtrade could be if scaled up. In the 1980s, there were 11,000 banana farmers in one island, Dominica. By the end of the 1990s, there were less than 700 as the islands, totally dependent on selling bananas to the UK, struggled to compete with cheap bananas from plantations in Latin America. The determined farmer Amos Wiltshire told me: 'The economy went down to zero because bananas are the heartbeat of the country. Everything was going haywire: increasing crime, youth violence, delinquency... Social chaos loomed.' Then the farmers started selling as Fairtrade and the situation has been totally turned around. Amos says: 'Fairtrade has been the saviour of the farmers in Dominica – of agriculture and the whole economy.' Farmers had hope again, and went back to their fields; they invested the premium in street lighting and sports clubs so bringing gang violence to an end.

Today, 3,600 farmers are in certified groups, representing 90 per cent of all banana farmers in the Windward Islands and nearly all their bananas are sold as Fairtrade, thanks to serious commitments by UK retailers. Next the farmers took more control of their supply chain, moving into exporting. Renwick Rose, from the Windward Islands Farmers' Association, said: 'For years farmers were considered the proverbial "hewers of wood and drawers of water", producing to the dictates and for the benefits of others. They were thought incapable of managing their own business. The transition to farmer control has demonstrated beyond the shadow of a doubt that farmers can do it for themselves.' Now the farmers face a new threat with changing EU banana rules... So the challenges always remain. But their unusual example gives an interesting insight into the potential of Fairtrade, if scaled up, to have a deeply significant impact on whole economies.

As the President of Rwanda, His Excellency Paul Kagame explained:

Fairtrade offers new opportunities for small-scale producers in Rwanda, and we have made great achievements in this respect, especially in the coffee industry. As a country where most people depend on agriculture, we must figure out how to move faster in this direction, in order to positively impact the economic well-being of rural communities.

IMPACT ON THE ENVIRONMENT

Fairtrade also impacts on the environment with strict standards for producers including the banning of some agrochemicals, minimised and safe use of others; proper and safe management of waste; maintenance of soil fertility and water resources; and no use of genetically modified organisms. One study found that in Guatemala non-Fairtrade farmers were almost twice as likely to use agrochemicals as Fairtrade farmers, while Jaffee's 2007 study[4] gives some wonderful examples of Mexican farmers cleaning up their coffee-processing which had been leaving rivers starved of oxygen. Many studies also record how the price and information have enabled farmers to convert to organic.

IMPACT ON THE PUBLIC

The FAIRTRADE Mark is now firmly established as the world's leading ethical consumer label. In the UK, more than seven out of ten members of the public recognise the mark and similar recognition rates are notched up across Europe, in some cases higher still.

In the UK, of those who buy Fairtrade products, more than 80 per cent rated the independent guarantee of the FAIRTRADE Mark as 'fairly' or 'very' important to them. Independent research has found that nine out of ten members of the public are aware of Fairtrade which is increasingly cited as the most effective way for them to play their part in tackling poverty.

At the heart of this growth in awareness has been one of Britain's most active grassroots social movements. The concept of Fairtrade towns has caught people's imagination, giving them a way to connect people's local actions in their village or city to the global fight against poverty, and 460 UK towns have already met the goals on awareness raising and availability of Fairtrade locally. The movement has been taken up by thousands of other groups – Fairtrade universities and colleges, faith groups and a relatively new Fairtrade schools scheme – and is now spreading across Europe, Australia, New Zealand and North America.

This locally rooted movement has helped bring the complex, distant issues of trade, development and poverty out to the wider public. Moreover it is deeply empowering – that word again. You do not need a PhD in trade policy, you only need to buy your Fairtrade tea and biscuits, and to chat about it at the school gate, to play your part in creating positive change. Now conditions for people growing the cotton in our clothes or the fruit in our juice are on the public agenda – and so the business agenda.

Of course the economic downturn has pushed people's own purses back into centre-stage. But the public have remained loyal to Fairtrade, showing the resilience of their desire for fairness. Indeed in 2009, sales grew over 12 per cent despite the recession, hitting an estimated retail value of £800 million for Fairtrade products in the UK. Across the global network, spanning 22 consumer countries, sales of Fairtrade reached the equivalent of £2.56 billion in 2008.

IMPACT ON BUSINESS

Years ago, Raul de Aguilas, a leading light in the Fairtrade movement from Peru, told me: 'To see the impact of Fairtrade, don't just look at our sales or market share, because Fairtrade has changed the agendas at every negotiating table. Many companies are not doing Fairtrade yet, but they are talking differently to us.'

As he said, Fairtrade's impact can be as great in changing business perceptions of how to add value, of what the public want and indeed of how they can engage differently with producers in their own supply chains. The growth in public awareness and consumer demand for Fairtrade has ignited commercial interest in Fairtrade. Because the public want Fairtrade, it makes commercial sense and can therefore be sustainable. In the UK alone some 440 businesses are licensed to sell Fairtrade products, with thousands engaged across the world. Public demand has allowed businesses to make big, bold decisions to commit to Fairtrade, has given businesses 'permission to care', and raised the bar on company engagement with producers in developing countries. So while all companies may not offer Fairtrade in part or whole, most companies are now looking at their supply chains and are aware that they cannot turn a blind eye to poor practice.

IMPACT ON GOVERNMENT

In December 2006, *The Economist* magazine wrote: 'The best thing about the spread of the ethical food movement is that it offers grounds for hope. It sends a signal that there is enormous appetite for change and widespread frustration that governments are not doing enough to preserve the environment, reform world trade or encourage development.'

Undoubtedly, the rising sales of Fairtrade are a clear message to successive governments that they have a public mandate to fight for fairer trade rules, in particular from the World Trade Organization. In addition, the fair trade movement has also sought to influence the policies of governments worldwide. In developing countries, Fairtrade producer groups have been able to demonstrate that access to markets and fair prices can stimulate rural growth and so lobby for increased support for smallholders. In developed countries, the public have pressed governments to ensure world trade rules are reformed in such a way that tackling poverty and promoting sustainable development are at their heart. The fair trade movement alone cannot of course hope to reach these ambitious goals. But it can and does play its part in helping governments hear the voices and see the needs of disadvantaged producers.

In conclusion, the movement still has everything to play for. When the early pioneers first struggled to get Fairtrade products from farmer to shopper, they could have had little idea of how far-reaching this new movement's impact could be. Our task now is to take this successful model, continue to adapt and improve it and also to extend radically its reach and impact. Worldwide, 2 billion people still earn less than $2 a day, many of them growing crops that people in rich countries enjoy every day. This is a scandal whose survival shames us all. That is why the Fairtrade movement is so determined to tip the balance of power in trade in favour of producers in developing countries. Turning that vision into reality will not be easy, especially as the global economy reels from recession. But fair trade is an extraordinary global movement, forming a unique alliance between millions of citizens across 80 countries, creating the living alternative that shows how trade can be fair. That legacy may be its greatest impact yet.

NOTES

1. Valerie Nelson and Barry Pound, *The Last Ten Years, A Comprehensive Review of the Literature on the Impact of Fairtrade*, National Resources Institute, September 2009, p. 7.
2. C. Dankers and P. Liu, *Environmental and Social Standards Certification and Labelling for Cash Crops*, Food and Agricultural Organization of the United Nations, 2003, p. 63.
3. L. Ronchi, *Monitoring of Fairtrade Initiatives*, Twin, 2002, p. 37.
4. D. Jaffee, *Brewing Justice: Fair Trade Coffee, Sustainability, and Survival*, University of California Press, 2007.

3
Rachel's Blog

Rachel Archer

I am going to introduce you to some of the inspiring people I have had the pleasure to meet over the last six years visiting farmers, workers and cooperative organisers in fair trade. They are just a few of a large and growing movement in different corners of the world, all linked by a desire to farm well, sell products for a fair and consistent price and improve conditions for their families and communities.

MARÍA'S MANGOES IN PERU

María Soveida de Mogollon is a tiny, delightful woman. A miniature tower of strength with fascinating hands – strong and twisted by years of work yet determined and incredibly smooth, she clasps them regularly and directs them purposefully to punctuate her speech. I first encountered her delivering her mangoes to the processing plant of the Apromalpi cooperative in December 2007.

As a member of the cooperative, María sells her Edward variety mangoes to be turned into puree and her Kent variety mangoes to be exported whole to organic Fairtrade markets.

María, 64, is the main breadwinner in her family since her husband's recent illness and death. I had a brief introduction to María before she returned to the more important task of ensuring her fruit was weighed correctly. At the busy processing plant I watched farmers, nearly all men, leaning on the wooden railings around a busy and chaotic scene, observing the weighing and loading of mangoes and discussing local news and politics. Amidst all of this, I noticed María stood quietly in the corner, never taking her eyes from her boxes of mangoes for the best part of two hours. Farmers here told me that before Apromalpi they used to be cheated on weight and price by local traders. Individual farmers had no bargaining power on price, so they sold at whatever price they were offered. Usually, the price was intolerably low. These practices die hard and now the farmers have their own cooperative, Apromalpi, to market their mangoes, they place due importance on supervising the sale of their mangoes, ensuring that the process is fair and that they hold their organisation to account. María explained to me:

> Building this mango processing plant has been a beautiful thing for us. I am very proud of what we have achieved. We, the farmer members of Apromalpi, have our own processing plant and nobody else has this. This is good for the local community too because it is generating jobs and I want there to be a legacy for our children and grandchildren.

The following day, I met María on her two hectares of land. We travelled out of the town of Chulacanas, along dirt tracks lined with wooden gates, passing an occasional pick-up truck but mostly people on foot, bicycle, motorbike taxi or donkeys and mules pulling carts piled high with maize or mangoes. María's land was a beautiful sanctuary of peace and tranquillity, with a cool breeze, hundreds of carefully tended mango trees, their branches heavily laden and bowing to the ground, and a shaded area for resting and boxing freshly picked mangoes. There was an air of calm yet evidence of years of dedicated hard work. 'My husband and I have always grown and sold mangoes,' María told me.

> We used to sell our mangoes through a local trader to Lima, but the prices were so terrible that they used to make us cry! The mangoes used to travel in the boot of a passenger bus to Lima. Things are a thousand times better with Apromalpi; it is a lovely situation to be in.

María cuts a fragile figure as she potters between the mango trees, yet I am struck by her stoicism and strength. 'My dream is to be able to add an extra storey to the house so that there is more room for all my family as our house is very cramped at the moment,' María explains.

> I hope that one day through selling my mangoes to the Fairtrade market I will achieve this. To people considering buying our mangoes in the shops, I must say that they are the best mangoes, because we've produced them in the best conditions and they are totally organic. Through Apromalpi and Fairtrade, we have more security and a better quality of life too.

FRESH ROOTS FOR JUAN IN THE DOMINICAN REPUBLIC

Visiting large banana growing regions can be an unsettling experience. Mile upon mile of banana plants stretch into the distance, with dusty tracks and deep drainage channels interspersed amongst them. The channels are often clogged with the plastic bags used to protect the growing bananas, and the water is a silty, sluggish, lifeless colour infested with mosquitoes. Missing is the beautiful and diverse wildlife of tropical countries and instead the poverty of the land is reflected in the poor, dirty conditions people often live in. The grim history of intensive production, enabled through heavy use of pesticides and fertilisers, is very evident. It is impossible not to consider the banana I have on my cereal each morning and feel ashamed at being part of this exploitative chain.

Fair trade banana farms provide a bit of a reprieve, amongst all this. Fairtrade standards have gone a long way towards improving the situation for farmers and workers by providing alternatives to many chemicals, banning aerial spraying whilst workers are in plantations and incorporating buffer zones around waterways to reduce contamination. Farmers I have met who are involved in fair trade have improved the way they farm and no longer suffer ailments caused by chemicals. What's more, they are participative, impassioned members of their cooperatives and communities.

In December 2008, I travelled to the Dominican Republic to visit a cooperative called Banelino, who have some new ideas about banana production. No matter what the climate or geography of a country, bananas are planted to the same rigid formula: a banana plant every one and a half metres with no other plants or crops to be seen. Travelling through the country's large traditional plantations I passed the familiar stark patterns of tall leaves and drainage trenches stretching for miles. But upon meeting farmer Juan Ramón García late one afternoon, standing amidst his one and a half hectares of lush green land, it was clear that he was set on finding a better way to farm. At first Juan Ramón seemed quiet and unassuming but it soon became clear that he was set on change. With a steady gaze he told me, 'I decided I wanted to be involved in implementing better things. I'm really happy

I joined the project because my production has improved a lot and it's more manageable because the land doesn't require as much water.'

The project began two years earlier as a biodiversity pilot involving a few of Banelino's 320 small banana farmer members. The ambitious objectives are to improve the environment, increase the productivity of the banana plants without the need for chemical fertilisers or pesticides, create additional work and income for the local community, and provide a model of best practice for other farmers to learn from.

We set off on our tour of Juan Ramón's banana plants and it was quite different from anything I had seen before. Juan Ramón had taken quite a risk by planting his bananas against the grain of convention: in rows with just one metre between plants but with three metres between each row. He had done so under the guidance of Gustavo Gandini, Banelino's infectiously enthusiastic environmental manager from Colombia. The three metre channels are planted with nitrogen-rich grass root peanuts, lemon and lime, papaya or cocoa trees. Not only do these plants and trees help to restore balance and nutrients to the soil, but they also provide an additional food source and income. Gandini explained, 'I don't want to see bare, exposed soil. This land should be covered with vegetation and full of life.' To show me the significance of this, he bent down and grabbed in both hands a random clod of moist earth at the foot of a banana plant. The soil was a rich brown colour and we counted four worms in it. The land is now teeming with them and there is no surer sign of health. Never before had I felt so excited about worms; this was such a contrast to the dried up, lifeless matter I had seen on other banana plantations. Gandini, stood in a channel of thigh high bean plants, is clearly delighted with the progress so far:

> Farmers truly understand the positive impact that this project is having on banana production. When they come and visit the plot and try to lift a stem of bananas – they buckle – it is so much heavier than they are used to! The idea is that farmers can visit these model plots, see the impact diversifying is having on the environment and the yield and apply these principles to improve their own farms.

This work is funded by a combination of international agencies and fair trade funds. It's a great example of how farmers who are organised attract development funding to bring about change. I felt inspired by this particular visit. It felt to me that small farmers are taking bananas into their own hands and discovering new ways to farm that could potentially improve the whole industry. Farmer Juan Ramón is now proudly at the cutting-edge of banana production.

SHRIMPS, FLOWERS AND BANANAS IN ECUADOR

A few months later I was with Angel Iñiguez and his family on their six hectare banana farm in Ecuador. Ecuador exports more bananas than any other nation and down on the flatlands, near to the coast, it is bleak and chemical ridden as a result. Here the small farmer cooperative of El Guabo was established in 1997, and became one of the first to become involved in fair trade. Angel explained its significance to me:

> It was too hard here before we joined El Guabo selling our bananas to intermediary buyers for whatever price they offered us. Sometimes we would get good prices, say seven dollars a box, but then prices

would fall as low as 80 cents a box. We were too small to sell to the big multinational companies; they only bought much bigger volumes directly from producers. For me fair trade is about selling a stable volume for a stable price and having health insurance.

Angel's farm was an oasis of green in the vast area of banana plantations we had just passed. He works there with his mother, father and sisters, pruning the banana plants and cutting down and packing bananas at their small washing and packing station. Beautiful wild red flowers flourish around the banana plants. And as we tramped through the dried banana leaves used as organic mulch, to find the fresh water stream running through the land, a couple of brightly coloured lizards scurried away. The stream was crystal clear and full of fish and shrimps, one of which Angel scooped up with a cut-off bottom of a plastic bottle. His face broke into a broad grin. We both knew that with conventional banana farming, the shrimps could never have survived. Angel explained, 'We like to care for the farm, to make it look beautiful so that it is a lovely place to be. It gives me great pleasure to see all the flowers amongst the bananas and to bring my daughter here to show her.'

Fellow farmer Abel described the environmental situation in more detail:

In the past, all of the trees were cut down so that the planes could fly overhead and drop the fungicides on the banana plants. We used a lot of pesticides and insecticides and lost the wildlife and insects. It was terrible because we were interrupting lifecycles and affecting the whole ecosystem. Our health also suffered. I used to have problems breathing, aches and pains and marks on my skin. Everything changed for us when we entered El Guabo. Fairtrade bans most of the agrochemicals and moves towards organic production. Since we became fully organic we have felt it financially because we used to produce 1,500 boxes of bananas a week but now we only produce around 900 boxes. I think consumers should know this and appreciate that it really is worth them paying a bit more for organic bananas. For me it is worth any sacrifices though because I live a healthy life here with my family. I also think Ecuador should be looked upon as the lungs of the Earth. We have the Amazon rainforest, the mountains and most people here live off the land. If more consumers are willing to buy organic and Fairtrade bananas, then the impact we have here on the environment would be less and people would be able to live more easily.

Prior to this trip, I associated buying organic produce with consumers firstly considering their own health and then the environment. But I came away inspired to buy only organic Fairtrade bananas, not so much because of my own health concerns, but because of the massive impact it has on the health of growers and their families as well as the environment.

FEISTY OLIVER AND COFFEE IN UGANDA

Oliver Kishero has a dazzling smile and a girly giggle. She is warm, enthusiastic and open. I have met her several times: in Uganda whilst visiting the coffee cooperative Gumutindo, of which she is a member; and in the UK, on a promotional tour for Cafédirect during Fairtrade Fortnight. She was delighted by the school children she met and horrified by most of the UK food, which was far too processed – 'Only the potatoes in Ireland are good,' she told me. In March 2007, I spent several days in her community, Buginyanya, in the hills of the majestic Mount Elgon, which straddles the border between Uganda and Kenya. We interviewed farmers together to use in a brochure to market Gumutindo's coffee to fair trade and organic coffee buyers. We trekked up and down bright red clay dirt tracks and across fields, me in wellies and soon flagging, and Oliver, in well-worn leather sandals and with boundless energy.

Those few days were a fascinating culture shock for me. It was a thriving community but very different from any I had experienced before. There was a great view from where I was staying across the valley of Buginyanya, where from sunrise women sang whilst they worked the fields in a long line, their babies strapped to their backs. There were no cars passing the small clay houses with rusty tin roofs, no electricity and no running water. The air was fresh and delicious with a tinge of wood smoke from all the cooking fires.

I quickly came to be amazed by the strength of women in that community. I passed many groups of women working the fields by hand. Others carried great sacks of fresh produce on their heads and backs, down to the local market several miles away. I learnt that traditionally, women work in the homes and on the land but despite this, have no economic or political power. The small plots of land are in their husband's name, and so their husbands are the breadwinners, despite their wives often doing the majority of the work. It is also culturally acceptable for men to have several wives. During the day, we visited a few circular drinking dens. Crowded and dim within, my eyes adjusted to the scene of men stooped around a central pot filled with a potent, home-brewed spirit. They each had a long straw stuck in the pot and steadily became more inebriated as they sat around discussing local politics, football and life. By no means were all men behaving in this way, but it seemed an acceptable norm.

Gumutindo coffee cooperative has focused on attracting farmer members who are committed to producing high quality coffee, and on the inclusion of women as members in their own right. Buginyanya was one of the first village-level cooperatives to join Gumutindo and its coffee is sold to fair trade and organic markets in Europe and the US. Oliver Kishero was amongst the first female coffee farmers to join and went on to be an international spokesperson for Gumutindo and the treasurer on its board.

I found myself quite in awe of Oliver's strength and vision. Her days are physical and long. In addition to tending her coffee, the main cash earner in the region, she prepares food three times a day for her family starting at sunrise, completely from scratch, over firewood in a smoke-filled hut. She has a vegetable patch, a clean stream running nearby, plantain, chickens and a couple of cows. Vegetables are uprooted and chopped plantain enters into a laborious process of peeling, steaming, wrapping and mashing to turn it into the Ugandan staple, *matoke*. Her husband, many years her senior and who she refers to as 'Mr Kishero', is a school teacher, who at the time of my visit was unemployed. They seemed to have a happy relationship and Oliver told me with relief that he had not taken another wife. But I certainly had the impression that it was Oliver who was the dynamic force within the partnership.

As we sat and peeled plantain outside Oliver's house, she told me more about her life:

> When I was younger, I wanted to be a teacher, but unfortunately, I lost my mother when I was 15 years old. I was then unable to attend school because I had to care for the younger ones. I wanted to be educated enough so that maybe I could be employed, but I didn't succeed in that. But I did say that when I am 50, I will not still be like

I was then. And I knew that this would need planning. So in 1989, I started to practise farming for myself. By the time Gumutindo came to Buginyanya, I was happy and proud because I had put all my efforts into my farm and now I could become a member. I have seven children. The main thing I wanted to be able to do was to educate them so that they do not have to be like me. My eldest daughter who is 16 tells me that she wants to be a doctor. I am paid more for my coffee now and so I can help her. I use my energy in my farm and I feel tired. I want them to have choices.

It seems that the overriding factor in motivating Oliver in farming has been a desire to help her children have more opportunities than she could ever have dreamt of. However, in the process she has become a role model for empowerment of women.

A TRIUMPHANT SURVIVOR: LUCIA IN NICARAGUA

Lucia always maintains an air of calm and order to her busy house. Grandchildren, children, friends, the travelling clothes salesman, and occasional tourists pass through her kitchen any time from dawn until well after dusk, as do chicks, puppies and the odd piglet, scavenging for food. She always has freshly-made tortillas, beans, salty cheese and strong, sweet coffee ready to offer her guests, or a swill bucket and dried maize for the animals. She has a solid build, honed to stand on her feet for a long time, and a warm face with honey skin and eyes that twinkle whenever she smiles or chuckles. She is a devout Catholic and enjoys singing along to the Catholic hymn hour on the battery-powered radio in the kitchen.

My partner and I recently lived with Lucia and her family in the northern coffee-growing region of Nicaragua. In the seven months we spent in the community it became so apparent to us how important and wide-reaching the benefits that cooperative farming and fair trade markets can bring. I decided this would be best explained by Lucia herself and so sat down with her one sunny morning to talk about how her life has changed.

Lucia is 59 years old but didn't believe she would live to see the day she turned 50. In the community of Sontule, in the mountains of northern Nicaragua, she lived under fear of being attacked by the Contra-revolutionary forces. Throughout the 1980s she spent most nights sleeping in the mountains with her children as the 'Contras' attacked several times killing and kidnapping members of the community. The community's 'crime' was that it had organised itself into a rural cooperative to farm the land after the landowner fled following the 1979 revolution. As a child, Lucia grew up in poverty, losing six of her 15 siblings in infancy through illnesses such as dysentery and gastric parasites. Lucia recalls:

My house as a child was made of sticks and mud, and the roof of grass. It had one bedroom. All of the biggest children slept in one bed. We slept without blankets, huddled together to keep warm. We were like chicks when the mother hen can no longer cover them.

When Lucia married her husband Rogelio at the age of 18, they owned nothing. It is with good reason then that Lucia is surprised by her survival to date and takes pride in her achievements. Today Lucia and Rogelio have six children and nine grandchildren and own around 15 hectares of land. They keep a few animals, and grow beans and corn to feed their family. They have a lovely home built of cement bricks with a tin roof. It has several bedrooms and a beautiful garden full of flowers and orange trees. Their main income is from coffee. Rogelio was one of the founding members of the village cooperative in the 1980s, and when peace returned to the countryside of Nicaragua in the 1990s, he encouraged Lucia to help set up the local women's cooperative, 'New Dawn'. Both cooperatives sell their coffee to organic and fair trade markets in Europe and the US.

The New Dawn cooperative collectively own around two hectares of land planted with coffee. It's not a lot, but it is significant as it is the first time the women have owned land in their own right. In its early days, the cooperative offered small loans to its members, who previously had never had access to credit. Some established small shops in their homes and others bought hens and sewing machines. Today, Lucia and many other women have organic vegetable patches, thanks to a scheme by a local organisation working through the cooperative to improve family diets in the countryside.

'We only ever ate what my father harvested when I was a child,' reflects Lucia.

> We would eat beans and tortillas most of the time. If there were no beans, then we would just eat tortillas with salt. I started to cook with lots of vegetables when we organised into the cooperative and I went to training sessions to learn to grow and cook them. I love to learn new recipes and to feed my family well.

The women have also received training sessions in gender, equality, leadership and self-esteem. Lucia explained their significance to me:

> After the war, I didn't believe it could really be over. I thought I was going to go crazy and didn't want to go out. It was only when we started to go to meetings that I began to slowly lose the trauma of the war. There is solidarity amongst the women here. Many of their

husbands did not want them to join the cooperative as they believed
women should stay at home and look after their children. They
thought that women might become rebellious. Some left, but some
fought to overcome it. The Revolution had shown us that women were
as brave as men. I am lucky, my husband has always wanted me to
be organised in a cooperative and has treated me well.

Some of the cooperative's most successful work has been
with external organisations in establishing a community-
tourism venture which has helped both economically and
socially. Lucia's daughter-in-law, Myra, who is also a member
of the cooperative, describes it:

We used to be too shy to say our names and introduce ourselves to
visitors, but now it feels like we have been re-born. We have better
conditions in our houses, thanks to the additional income and we
have gained in lots of experiences and enjoy receiving international
visitors. We have also made links with educational institutions in the
US who are supporting our children with scholarships to study beyond
primary school.

Lucia continues:

Coffee prices have been a lot better since the 1990s thanks to the
cooperatives so we've been able to achieve more. The main thing
has been the education of our children. If the prices are low, we
can't help with studying. We also have some social benefits through
Fairtrade, like school equipment for children, medicines and some
training. It is so different to my childhood. Back then my parents
said it wasn't necessary for girls to study. I felt ashamed growing up
without learning to read or write, not being able to sign my name,
or read an invitation.

Lucia and her family at times have suffered hardships and
anguish in their lives on a scale that is difficult to imagine.

But they have also been presented with opportunities: to join cooperatives, to learn to read and write as adults following the revolution, to buy land, to attend feminist workshops, to grow vegetables, and to participate in the tourism venture. They have embraced these projects and incorporated them into creating a better quality of life for themselves, their family and their community. Fair trade plays a role in all of this. It has enabled markets for their cooperatives to thrive in, enabled them to capitalise and buy infrastructure so that they are owners of the coffee supply chain. Crucially, it has enabled them to remain organised, this means so much here as in addition to better markets and community solidarity, they also attract more project funding and investment. It is a community which is actively striving for better things.

No farmer I have ever met in Africa, Latin America or the Caribbean has just talked about him or herself as an individual. They see themselves as part of a movement to improve conditions for their families, their communities and for the environment. For me, this is what the fair trade movement is essentially about.

4
Nicaragua:
The Road to Freedom

Pedro Haslam and Nicholas Hoskyns

ROOTS IN REVOLUTION

Nicaragua's revolution triumphed on 19 July 1979. The Sandinistas came to power having overthrown the Somoza dictatorship. The revolution won the hearts of the vast majority of Nicaraguans and caught the imagination of the world. In the initial years there were huge and rapid advances in education, health and importantly for this chapter an extensive and successful land reform from 1980 to 1988 where valuable lands were given to the *campesinos* organised in cooperatives.

In response to this exciting revolutionary model in Central America, the newly elected US government presided over by Ronald Reagan financed the Contra war and imposed an economic embargo on Nicaragua. This ugly period in US foreign policy, known as the Iran–Contra scandal, came to light when the US was found to have funded the Contra war through revenues from illegal arms sales to Iran. In 1986 the International Court of Justice ruled in favour of Nicaragua that the United States acted illegally.[1]

In response to the external aggression the Nicaraguan people had no choice but to change from organising brigades to teach people to read and write to organising brigades to defend their lives and the revolution. The first line of defence in the countryside was the recently formed cooperatives who endured the full force of the Contras' attacks. The phenomenal developments that were being achieved in production and social development were nipped in the bud in a most cruel way.

Spontaneously an international movement in solidarity with the Nicaraguan people developed. Thousands of volunteers headed to Nicaragua to build schools and houses and to pick coffee, often in communities in the war zone where the Contras had wielded their destruction. The international solidarity movement with Nicaragua was creative and full of hope. The first shipment of bananas left for Belgium in May 1985, just two days before the US embargo began, and shipments continued throughout the Contra war. This new solidarity market of Europe was small but symbolically very significant. In the United States sympathisers were also making a stand against the blockade. Taking advantage of a loophole in the blockade Jonathan Rosenthal of Equal Exchange, a pioneer worker cooperative, imported roasted Nicaraguan coffee from Holland. At the same time a small US roaster, Paul Katzeff, took Nicaraguan coffee to Canada where it was roasted and imported from there to be sold as 'Cafe Por La Paz' (Peace Coffee). Paul Katzeff went even further and sued Ronald Reagan for illegally preventing him from purchasing Nicaraguan coffee directly. The case was taken to the second highest court in the country before the process was derailed by a law change in Congress. These initiatives motivated by politics and solidarity were among the first expressions of fair trade in the world. Many of these first visionaries continue to lead initiatives within the fair trade and solidarity movements today.

In 1990 the Sandinistas lost the elections in Nicaragua and on 10 January 1991 peacefully handed over power to the US-backed rightwing coalition. Violeta Chamorro became President and her government imposed neo-liberal policies that put many of the achievements of the revolution in danger. Free healthcare and education came under threat as did the land reform, which had redistributed 20 per cent of the country's total arable land and significantly raised production levels.[2] Her government actively promoted the devolution of these lands to the former owners, many of whom had become US citizens while in exile and had the full backing of the US embassy for their demands. The campesinos were in a very difficult situation, lacking access to markets and credit. Their land titles, which had not been completely legalised, were under threat. Many cooperatives dissolved and large numbers of the small farmers sold their lands in desperation at well below market values.

It is in this context that, in the early 1990s, a new wave of cooperatives were formed. The driving force behind them was the need for the campesinos to defend their lands and gain access to markets and finance. Fair trade gave this generation of cooperatives the opportunity to export their coffee directly. The campesinos sold for higher prices and the cooperatives were able to compete successfully with the private exporters. Very soon the small farmers were purchasing processing plants and managing small loan funds to finance production. The farmers were gaining control of the production chain that had been inaccessible to them in the traditional agro-business model.

Many people throughout the world who work in fair trade have been inspired by the Nicaraguan experience. Anita Roddick, founder of the Body Shop, wrote on the 25th anniversary of the Nicaraguan revolution:

> Nicaragua has a special place in my heart. This tiny country overthrew a brutal dictator in a popular revolution in 1979 only to face a long, bloody civil war provoked and then sustained by Ronald Reagan and the United States covertly illegally and in defiance of the country's own congress. I went to Nicaragua in 2001, a decade after the end of the revolution and the contra war. I stayed in the northern hills with the farming cooperatives of Achuapa that is a community trade supplier of sesame oil to the Body Shop... wherever I went I met amazing, organized and committed people. For all the hardships Nicaraguans have endured and the efforts of successive right wing governments to dismantle the social apparatus of the revolution, the spirit lives on![3]

Anita tragically died in September 2007 and we lost a great friend and activist.

More than 30,000 people died in the war in Nicaragua during the 1980s fighting for what they believed in. Our roots lie in the struggle for a more just world. Our strength lies in us not being alone.

RAPID GROWTH (1990–98)

Globally the fair trade movement grew fast both in numbers and in influence. New products were certified, and national initiatives in consumer countries came together to form a single international mark under FLO, Fairtrade Labelling Organizations International. The independent certification body FLO-Cert was also created. The farmers were participating in forums, consultation groups and travelling all over the world participating in this new trading system and promoting their products.

The cooperatives' successes were achieved despite the coffee crisis that was triggered by the collapse of the International Coffee Agreement in 1989. During the crisis, the fair trade minimum remained stable at $126 per 100lb including a $5 social premium while coffee not sold to the fair trade market fell below $50 per 100lb. The whole Nicaraguan coffee sector suffered and six banks collapsed partly because of the $300 million of bad coffee debt. The most severely affected were the coffee labourers who no longer had employment. Three years in succession they protested, marching down from the mountains to block the Pan-American Highway on their way to Managua. They won concessions from the Nicaraguan government of which the most important was being given land at concessionary prices. They formed cooperatives and many are now producing and exporting their own coffee, others are back working as coffee labourers on the plantations.

Even through the coffee crisis the fair trade movement was accomplishing what everyone had said was impossible. This was to a large extent due to the incredible network of friends, acquaintances and business partners that had been built up across the globe. The strength of the network was founded on the highest social and environmental ethics and an incredible level of mutual respect and trust, which was the foundation for the explosion of innovations that were underway.

In Nicaragua the fair trade market expanded quickly to include sesame seeds. The initial markets were the Body Shop from Britain and Oxfam Werdewinkels in Belgium who both still purchase today. Sesame oil was developed in a small cooperative in Achuapa, northern Leon and later the second level sesame cooperative Del Campo became the first fair trade certified sesame cooperative in the world. The community trade criteria developed with the Body Shop became the basis for the fair trade standards.

Also in the 1990s Twin Trading in the UK led by Albert Tucker made Cafédirect into the most successful 100% fair trade brand, and Divine Chocolate followed close behind. Two cooperatives both named Equal Exchange, one in Scotland and the other in the US, both developed their 100% fair trade brands against all the odds. Oxfam Werdewinkels in Belgium grew to over 200 outlets relying heavily on volunteers, some of whom were the very same people who initiated the sale of Nicaraguan bananas to Europe during the 1980s.

The international fair trade network inspired an initiative in Nicaragua to build the first cupping labs for and owned by small farmers. Cupping Laboratories are fully equipped tasting rooms where trained coffee tasters called 'cuppers' slurp and rate coffee samples. The idea to give farmers access to this elite process was proposed by Paul Katzeff. It was 1998 and Paul had just become president of the Specialty Coffee Association of America. The proposal was simple but far reaching: if the small farmers could taste their own coffees, 'know the target' of coffee quality and speak the language of coffee buyers, they would be able to improve the quality of their coffees and sell to small coffee roasters directly.

The international fair trade network brought nine of the best cooperatives together, many of whom were already exporting coffee to the fair trade market, but who were not experts in quality. When the cooperatives were presented with the idea they incorporated the labs into their own plans and dreams and immediately began choosing the most beautiful woods to make their cupping tables and selecting their brightest stars to be trained as cuppers. Nine unique cupping labs were built throughout Nicaragua's coffee country, all of which are still working today.

The cupping labs exceeded all expectations, as deal after deal was done directly with coffee roasters, some of whom made Nicaragua their first visit to a producer country. Not only did they commit to buying the coffees there and then, but price suddenly became secondary and the focus shifted to the families and communities who produced the coffee. A new way of business resulted, negotiating in the cupping labs and then visiting the farmers. The coffee buyers naturally decided to become more involved with the communities they visited, often offering to finance social and environmental projects as well as directly investing in coffee quality improvement. The roasters had unforgettable experiences that they immediately incorporated into their marketing. Nicaraguan single origin coffees became prominent all over the US with the stories of the families and communities who produced them enhancing the coffee experience for the drinker. Cupping lab fever took over the coffee industry in Nicaragua, and labs sprang up at more cooperatives and private exporters. The importers became observers as their role was changing from the indispensable middleman to becoming providers of finance and mere organisers of the logistics of importing the coffee.

The model was so attractive and powerful that within a very few years it was replicated in some form or other in nearly every coffee-producing country in the world. We saw a rapid change in the way coffee, the second largest traded product in the world, was bought and sold with the power shifting towards the farmer and the small roaster and away from the large importer and corporation.

FRUITS OF SUCCESS AT THE PEAK OF EMPOWERMENT
(1998–2004)

From the Nicaraguan perspective the fair trade movement peaked from 1998 to 2004. A united empowered movement was changing the way products were traded in the world. Small farmer cooperatives in southern producing countries were linking up with successful 'Alternative Trading Organisations' (ATOs) in the northern consuming countries and using all of their combined knowledge, experience and resources to make trade fairer. In Nicaragua the cooperatives described a 'quality exchange', where high quality products for consumers provided for an improved quality of life for the farmer families and their communities.

The small farmers in Nicaragua had become owners of whole production chains up to export. This empowered cooperative movement was young and vibrant and was a real alternative to the traditional exploitative agro-export model.

The small farmers were now exporting over 20 per cent of Nicaragua's coffee and over 50 per cent of the country's sesame directly through their cooperatives. Strong second level cooperatives were established all over the country. Part of the sector's great strength was its diversity. This occurred because all the cooperatives grew independently and only came together to coordinate once they were already well established.

The 'Central de Cooperativas de Servicios Multiples' (PRODECOOP), based in Esteli, is a good illustration of how to bring 2,400 of the smallest coffee farmers together. They have built one of the most beautiful processing plants in the country, achieved the very best prices for their members and have had winning coffees in the most renowned international coffee competition 'The Cup of Excellence' every year since its initiation in 2002. In 2005 Prodecoop won the first place coffee with a certified organic fair trade coffee. It is important to note the very high profile of women within the Nicaraguan cooperative movement, among them the general manager of Prodecoop, Merling Presa, who is also the first coordinator of the Latin American Network of Fair Trade Cooperatives (CLAC).

The 'Central de Cooperativas del Norte R.L.' (CECOCAFEN) is based in Matagalpa. And a true pioneer of the new cooperative business model in Nicaragua, drawing its strength from a clear ideological position defending the small farmers, their families and the communities from the ravishes of rampant capitalism. Cecocafen represents 2,200 small coffee farmers and has successfully integrated them into the whole coffee chain. It has a renowned women's savings programme, and is promoting rural eco-tourism as well as environmental protection projects. It also provides grants to support youths right through to university. A member cooperative in San Ramon has recently built over 100 homes for its associates. Martha Villareyna, the general manager of Cecocafen, was raised in the rural village of San Ramon and now is a pillar of strength in the Nicaraguan cooperative movement.

The 'Union de Cooperativas Agropecuarias' (SOPPEXCCA) is a second level cooperative based in Jinotega. Fatima Ismael Espinosa has been its manager since its founding. She is one of the most well-respected farmer leaders in the fair trade movement. For her the biggest achievement of Soppexcca has been to keep the small farmers working and owning their land. Soppexcca also excels in addressing gender inequality and youth involvement. Women receive support and training in an integral women's programme. They are supported in reproductive health issues and have preferential access to credit. They have taken up prominent leadership roles within the cooperative and promoted the sale of 'Women's Coffee' grown only by women. Soppexcca manages 180 grants for youth at all levels of education, and promotes art, music and dance groups. Four rural communities have been declared free of school absenteeism through an initiative promoted by the cooperative. Soppexcca continues to be a shining example of what an organised community can achieve through fair pricing and agricultural trade.

The 'Central de Cooperativas de Importacion y Exportacion' (DEL CAMPO), based in Leon, has become the largest sesame exporter in Nicaragua, selling the highest quality hulled seed and single variety natural seed to Japan. It has pioneered both certified fair trade and organic sesame. Del Campo has built a state-of-the-art sesame hulling plant and operates one of the best traceability systems in Nicaragua. Its cooperatives have many social projects, such as the annual international music and solidarity festival run in August every year in Achuapa, the most isolated municipality of Leon. Originally from Achuapa, Juan Bravo is the president of Del Campo and also the manager of the new national 'Federation of Agro-industrial Cooperatives' (FENIAGRO). Del Campo along with Cecocafen is a founder of Etico, a new UK-based company owned by charities and cooperatives that enables the farmers to sell sesame and coffee products directly to small end users in Europe and the US.

The Nicaraguan small farmer cooperative sector is now working at a national level to leverage groundbreaking financial deals in favour of small farmers and participating in shaping the international movement through CLAC and the Fairtrade Labelling Organizations International (FLO). Nicaraguan farmers are also sitting on the boards of fair trade companies in the north.

THE PAINS OF SUCCESS (2004–09)

The reaction from the large traditional companies was quick in coming. After ridiculing fair trade since its inception they suddenly wanted in. For those of us who had founded fair trade as a tool for social change and revolution it felt like betrayal. Despite considerable resistance, profound heart searching and debate they were included and started stacking their certified fair trade products onto the shelves.

The list of those now certified to sell fair trade products is notable. In the north companies such as Starbucks, Nestlé, Sainsbury's, Tesco, Wal-Mart and McDonald's were signed up. These are the very companies that many fair trade consumers avoid purchasing from, based on accusations of not upholding general fair trade and labour values. Their business practice histories indicate that their motivations for signing up to fair trade are based on marketing success rather than ideology.

In Nicaragua transnational exporters such as Atlantic and Volcafe who compete directly with the cooperatives have also been certified. The fair trade certified farmers who sell to them are back to being just farmers organised in first level cooperatives, and are still locked into the traditional supply chains dominated by the largest companies. This is not the vision of sustainability and community many of us started out with, where local family-owned businesses sell the products of small farmers and personal relationships are maintained throughout the supply chain.

Fair trade has changed from a movement that effectively contributes to empowerment, social change and economic justice to one that is also effectively improving the image of some of the most mistrusted companies in the world. As a result of the debate surrounding the inclusion of multinationals and plantations the fair trade movement became divided and lost the unity of a shared vision. Instead the key players in fair trade have fragmented into many directions, in some ways setting the stage for the next wave of innovative fair trade developments.

THE NEXT WAVE (2007–PRESENT)

Just like in nature, in social movements the next wave is always just behind the one that has reared its beautiful crest. As we have highlighted, women's groups are developing within the cooperatives, some buyers are giving additional payments in recognition of the unpaid work of women and there are supply chains solely owned by the small farmers right up to the point of export. Complete transparency and traceability have been achieved within the cooperative owned chains including calculations of carbon footprint cycles. Ownership of the supply chain is also fertile terrain for development with farmer cooperatives owning shares in northern ATOs such as Cafédirect, Liberation and Etico in the UK and Equal Exchange in the US. However, there is one initiative that is truly taking fair trade to the next level and that is the 'Alianza Bolivariana para los Pueblos de Nuestra America' (ALBA).

ALBA in English is the 'Bolivarian Alliance for Peoples of the Americas' and was initially formed in reaction to the free trade agreement for the Americas promoted by the US and its allies in Latin America (ALCA). Nicaragua became a full member immediately after the Sandinistas returned to government on 10 January 2007, after 16 years of being in opposition. The current full members of ALBA are Venezuela, Cuba, Bolivia, Nicaragua, Ecuador, Dominican Republic, Antigua and Barbados, Saint Vincent and the Grenadines. Honduras was a full member until the recent military coup ousted the democratically elected president Manuel Zelaya. ALBA energetically denounced the situation in Honduras and is a strong voice on the international stage.

ALBA has declared itself committed to fair trade 'Comercio Justo' and Food Security. It has an integral and optimistic vision of what can be achieved based on local and south–south trade. Its objective is to transfer the benefits to the disadvantaged, concentrating both on small farmers and low-income consumers. It dovetails fair trade with food security and empowerment. In Nicaragua for example, support is given to the small farmers to produce rice, beans, maize and to raise cattle primarily for the local market, with minimum prices guaranteed by the state owned basic grains company ENABAS. Any excess is then available for export to other ALBA countries, mainly Venezuela.

Fair trade Nicaraguan exports to Venezuela started in 2008 when $27 million was exported, in 2009 exports rose dramatically to $109 million and projections for 2010 are $239 million. Nicaragua is currently exporting meat, beans and more recently coffee under ALBA fair trade terms. In coffee, the very cooperatives that initiated fair trade are using their expertise and processing facilities to supply Venezuela.

The value of coffee sales in 2010 is expected to be between $25 million and $40 million. Minimum prices are established before guaranteed quantities are contracted. Priority is given to the small farmers and the cooperatives and there are short, medium and long term goals, which include the building of state-of-the-art processing plants. Advance payments are given to the cooperatives and a long term commitment and strategic plan is being developed which includes $10 million for financing small farmers in 2011. Not only has ALBA contributed to a 31.83 per cent overall increase in Nicaraguan exports in the first third of 2010, but the trade standards show an impressive commitment to fair trade and equality.[4]

CONCLUSION

In Nicaragua revolution and land reform allowed a successful small farmer empowered cooperative sector to develop, with access to international markets. The solidarity movement with Nicaragua, that incorporated trade as a tool for activism, has truly changed the world. Their courage along with the pioneer work of Nicaraguan farmers initiated fair trade as we know it today. Together we have proven that fair trade can make a significant difference to the world. The cupping labs at the cooperatives put farmers, importers and roasters on equal footing. Women have flourished within the cooperatives as farmers and as leaders.

When our work was surprisingly validated by large transnational companies most us struggled to incorporate them into our mindset of fair trade. After much debating many of us have refocused, and the quest for empowerment, sustainability and social change once again has no limits. There is no prescribed formula, only the proof that we can harvest sweet fruits of success when we work together with a shared vision. ALBA has embraced fair trade and made Latin America the stage. For the first time fair trade is being incorporated into state policy with large-scale optimistic long term strategies including food security. Fair trade is no longer just exports to wealthy countries where consumption is primarily by affluent consumers. Some of the fastest growth is in the sale of rice, beans, meat and maize within ALBA.

When we started, the goal of empowering small farmers seemed impossible to achieve, but we knew we had to do something. Albert Tucker likes to talk about 'jumping off cliffs', Paul Katzeff speaks of reorganising structures and Anita Roddick considered herself an 'Activist' with her funeral specifically celebrating that fact. We in Nicaragua still proudly refer to revolution. Others talk of caring, following your heart and doing your duty. Whatever it is or however we like to describe it, it is about striving to contribute to a better world through concrete actions.

One day in the future, we will look back and ask: 'Why was trade ever unfair?'

NOTES

1. *The Republic of Nicaragua* v. *The United States of America* was a 1986 case of the International Court of Justice (ICJ) in which the ICJ ruled that the US had violated international law by supporting Contra guerrillas in their rebellion against the Nicaraguan government and by mining Nicaragua's harbours. The United States refused to participate in the proceedings after the court rejected its arguments that the ICJ lacked jurisdiction to hear the case. The US

later blocked enforcement of the judgment by the United Nations Security Council and thereby prevented Nicaragua from obtaining any compensation.

2. Tom Barry, *Roots of Rebellion: Land and Hunger in Central America*, South End Press, Boston, US, 1987, pp. 105–36.
3. Anita Roddick, personal note published on her website, www.anitaroddick.com
4. Managua/ACAN-EFE, 'Cetrex: Exportaciones Aumentan en 32.4%', *La Prensa*, 6 April 2010, www.laprensa.com.ni/2010/04/06/economia/21084

5
Heroes and Demons

Jeroen Kroezen

I first met Jorge Ramirez in January 1998. I was living in Quito at the time and flew down to Guayaquil; the big, chaotic, hot and dusty harbour city on Ecuador's Pacific coast. From there I took a collective taxi, a yellow Chevrolet from the eighties, and embarked on a six hour journey along a pothole stricken road to Machala, the 'banana capital of the world'.

I checked into the hotel Rizzo, where the corporate rate of $15 a night was reflected in the flaky paint work and worn out sheets. The hotel was close to the office of ExpoEcoAgro, a small and young banana company which I visited the following day.

Raul Ituralde, a former priest, was the manager of ExpoEcoAgro and he explained the difficulties the company was having. El Niño[1] was causing severe damage to the banana plantations and, as a result, there was a shortage of quality fruit. This, in turn, was presenting him with a 'dead freight'[2] issue which was putting severe pressure on the business.

While we were speaking Jorge Ramirez arrived and joined the meeting. Jorge had a very friendly and peaceful appearance. He had a pronounced nose and soft eyes, reminding me of paintings of Inca leaders from centuries ago. He spoke softly and chose his words carefully and, when he spoke, people listened. Jorge was the leader of one of the groups of banana producers who were supplying ExpoEcoAgro. He was not at all the person I expected him to be. Jorge was an educated man who spoke clearly, made careful analyses and was able to explain things in an analytical way.

No sooner had Jorge joined the meeting when there was a sudden commotion. Somebody was screaming at Raul to look out of the window. He jumped up to see two guys transferring the spare wheel from his car into theirs. Raul went to his desk and took a pistol from the drawer. He fired three bullets at the roof of the car that was driving away at high speed. It all happened in a few seconds and I just sat there flabbergasted. This was my welcome to Machala, a city with the self-proclaimed title 'Capital Mundial de Banano'.

BANANA WARS

Machala may be the hub of a multi-billion dollar banana industry but, as a city, it is characterised by bad and small roads, many just of dirt, houses which are only half built; a dusty place without parks or trees. As you enter the city you run into a roundabout with the statue of a worker struggling under the weight of a huge branch of bananas. This symbolises the history of the banana industry in Ecuador and the rest of South and Central America.

In his book about the history of bananas Peter Chapman relates how the United Fruit Company was regularly accused of bribing Latin American government officials in order to secure preferential treatment, exploiting workers, misusing monopoly power, and actively encouraging coups against smaller nations to secure dictatorships which supported the company's commercial interests. In 1911 it was involved in a coup which installed General Manuel Bonilla as the president of Honduras. Similarly, there was strong evidence of its involvement when Jacobo Arbenz was deposed as president of Guatemala in 1954.[3]

There is a temptation to think of the well-publicised abuses of banana workers in the southern hemisphere as something from the past; a problem for a different generation which has since been resolved. But this is far from being the case. In 2002 1,400 workers on the Noboa plantations in Ecuador attempted to organise themselves into a union. They wanted recognition of the union, their legal right to healthcare, and higher wages; their average wage was less than the legal minimum. When the company refused their demands a strike ensued. The company hired 200 men to break up the perfectly legal strike. The violence left 19 injured and one man without his leg.[4] Perhaps little wonder then that Raul Ituralde kept a loaded pistol in the drawer of his desk.

THE ECUADORIAN BANANA SECTOR

The many small and medium sized banana producers from Ecuador can stay in business because of favourable climatic circumstances for bananas. The cold Humbolt current from the south passes Ecuador's coast and the resultant low winter temperatures act as a natural control on Black Sigatoka, the main disease that attacks bananas. As a result Ecuador has become the world's banana reserve; the main spot market with extremely volatile prices.

For decades the Ecuadorian government has tried to regulate prices by defining a minimum price which should be respected by exporters and the middlemen who buy directly from producers. But the government does not have the instruments to enforce this policy and the large companies have used many tricks to avoid the minimum price. For example, they might deduct a bogus service charge from the payments they make to producers. Small producers feel unable to complain because they fear being blacklisted by the exporters.

The exporters are also vulnerable. They are dependent on the market prices in Europe and North America; often shipping the fruit without any agreed price. They are also subject to claims back on them from importers if the quality on arrival fails to meet exacting specifications. This process lacks transparency as importers can use it to transfer the risk back to the exporters if market conditions are tough and sales difficult.

The importers are increasingly dependent on the major supermarket groups. Contracts between suppliers and retailers are quite rare. This means that supermarkets often present short term orders to their suppliers and expect them to deliver. If they need fewer bananas than anticipated they don't take responsibility for the excess volumes.

FAIRTRADE BANANAS IN ECUADOR

It was a Dutch guy named Bert Beekman, contracted by the Dutch NGO Solidaridad, who travelled to Ecuador to develop a Fairtrade plan for bananas. Solidaridad had established Fairtrade in the coffee sector and, after failing to persuade the major multinational companies to back the banana plans, went out to look for smaller players who might support this thinking. These efforts resulted in the establishment of a new company called ExpoEcoAgro. This was, in effect, a cooperation between a regional group of small banana producers (UROCAL), its leaders and managers (Desagro), and Solidaridad, the Dutch ecumenical development agency. Solidaridad was in partnership with SNV Ecuador; a Dutch development organisation that I worked for to support the Fairtrade banana project.

The first major hurdle was the need to access shipping. The banana business is built on regular weekly shipping to Europe and most of the ships are owned and controlled by the major banana companies. So the new venture entered into an alliance with Bananor, an Ecuadorian export company owned by some large and wealthy banana producers. As part of the agreement Bananor was also allowed to supply Fairtrade by producing 50 per cent of the Fairtrade volumes. The operation started in November 1996 with the export of OKE branded Fairtrade bananas for the Dutch market.

But the path to success rarely runs smoothly. By the time I arrived on the scene, at the beginning of 1998, sales had been extended into Denmark, Belgium and Switzerland but volumes were small and the organisation of farmers hardly existed. UROCAL had failed to recruit the number of farmers anticipated. Only the group from the village of El Guabo had been effectively organised and, according to Jorge Ramirez, its leader, this had been done without the support of UROCAL.

There were also tensions in the 'boardroom'. The plan had been for the farmers to become the majority shareholder, with the shares gifted by Solidaridad, but UROCAL had been reluctant to work towards empowering the farmers; they wanted to have full control over the business and, behind the backs of their partners in ExpoEcoAgro, had started the parallel export of 'ethical bananas' to Germany.

Nor was the relationship with Bananor running smoothly. The management of Bananor were experienced banana traders and continuous issues on volumes, payments, quality requirements, and claims had undermined trust in the relationship.

To cap it all El Niño arrived. The Ecuadorian banana industry was not prepared for the rains. Many plantations flooded. Roads and bridges were damaged. The producers could not deliver the volumes and so exports were cut back. The quality of bananas deteriorated as the exposure to excess water resulted in ripening and rotting during transit. Dead freight and quality claims from importers in Europe and North America started to hit the exporters. ExpoEcoAgro had to pay around $500,000 in quality claims.

THE BIRTH OF AGROFAIR

Solidaridad established Max Havelaar, the first Fairtrade label, and introduced Fairtrade coffee in 1988. Committed to the promotion of social justice it devised a five point master plan to extend Fairtrade into the banana sector:

- Establish a new import company in Europe (AgroFair) to focus on the development of a Fairtrade market for bananas.
- Develop a source of Fairtrade bananas in Ecuador.
- Develop a source of Fairtrade bananas in Ghana – Costa Rica was added later as a third source.

- Persuade the Dutch retail industry to stock Fairtrade by a major promotion of OKE bananas in 1996.
- Create access for Fairtrade bananas into Europe, a market which had been heavily protected through trade barriers.

Conscious of the years of exploitation suffered by farmers and workers at the hands of the major multinational businesses Solidaridad wanted to introduce Fairtrade bananas to the world. Their initial approach was to talk to the major companies who had been primarily responsible for most of the injustice and who still dominated the world banana trade. But these multinational companies saw Fairtrade as an unnecessary headache which they preferred to avoid. Not to be deterred Nico Roozen, the director of Solidaridad, decided it would found its own banana company in order to turn the vision into reality.

AgroFair Benelux, based in Holland, was born in 1996. It linked up with Volta River Exports Ltd (VREL) in Ghana to establish the first Fairtrade certified plantation in the world. For Ecuador, Solidaridad engaged the services of Bert Beekman to develop a plan for the supply of Fairtrade bananas.

THE EUROPEAN UNION AND IMPORT BARRIERS

Ever since the establishment of a single European market in 1993, the importing of bananas into the European Union had been a controversial issue. The former colonies of the European member states wanted to maintain their preferential market access to the UK (Windward Islands, Jamaica and

Belize), Holland (Surinam) and France (Cameroon and Côte d'Ivoire). This resulted in an enormous lobby which, combined with a sense of colonial guilt, ended up with one of the most controversial trade barriers in history. In order to bring bananas into Europe an importer needed a quota for a specific country. The former colonies enjoyed quotas which were bigger than their production volumes, in effect allowing them free entry into the European market. Bananas from South America, often referred to as Dollar bananas, had very tight quotas and also had to pay a tariff on entry into the market. The Latin American countries were furious. The system was demonstrably unfair.

To make matters worse the quotas were distributed between European importers on the basis of historical volumes. This meant that new companies were effectively blocked from the market. Clearly this was a major problem for the infant AgroFair. Fortunately the new company had established a relationship with a German importer called T-Port. The initial intention had been for T-Port to take a shareholding in AgroFair but this failed to materialise as they did not want to enter as a minority shareholder. Nevertheless good relations had been maintained and T-Port agreed to use its own quota to buy the Fairtrade bananas into Europe, selling them to AgroFair.

EL GUABO

These developments had major implications for the nascent Fairtrade business in Ecuador. But in May 1998, in the wake of El Niño, the export of Fairtrade bananas to Europe stopped. The shipping line from T-Port suspended its operations as there were not sufficient bananas to fill the ships. ExpoEcoAgro had serious debts and had ceased operations. The initial plan had failed.

The only hope of getting things back on track was Jorge Ramirez and the El Guabo farmers association. He believed in the concept and believed that it could work. And so did I. We simply had to wind down the existing company and start again. We needed a legal entity registered as an exporter, we needed shipping, we needed production and we needed packing materials.

As a result of the crisis, AgroFair had developed a new source for Fairtrade bananas in Costa Rica. This meant that the need for Ecuadorian bananas was not so evident. Solidaridad was reluctant to invest further time and money as confidence in the quality was now weak. But Leen Paardekooper, director at AgroFair, believed there might be possibilities in Switzerland. The Swiss had a preference for Ecuadorian bananas and, as Switzerland was not part of the European Union, no import quotas were required.

Working from the ground floor of Jorge's house we registered the El Guabo Farmers Association as an exporter. This was far from straightforward as we were an association and not a limited company. We had meetings with the farmers at weekends in order to get their support for a new start. The initial payment we were going to receive from AgroFair would not cover all of our costs and so we asked the farmers to supply the fruit without the security that they were going to get paid. It was due to the inspirational leadership of Jorge, in combination with my independent status, which helped persuade the farmers to go out on a limb. It turned out to be the key for future success. The farmers experienced the shipment as their shipment. It was their bananas, their export, their business, and their risk. The feeling of ownership made the difference.

The first container was ordered alongside the football pitch in El Guabo. Wilson Navarette, secretary of the association, was coordinating the planning and loading of the container. Normally the farmers had to deliver their bananas with small trucks to the harbour at Puerto Bolivar, close to Machala. But now they had to deliver their bananas in the village of El Guabo. We organised a last quality control check next to the container. Some of the boxes from each farmer were opened and examined by an experienced inspector. A new and unexpected development took place. Normally farmers are only interested in getting their own fruit through quality control. But now they were interested in the quality of the other farmers. They realised that this was their own shipment and if other farmers delivered poor quality it was going to adversely affect each of them.

The first container was despatched to Switzerland in October 1998. The container was a success. The quality was excellent. In January 1999 we started shipping three to four containers a week.

THE FURTHER DEVELOPMENT OF EL GUABO

The successful development of a banana programme with European retailers requires a secure and consistent weekly delivery programme. So when El Guabo's exports were interrupted several times during 1999 this represented a major problem. The difficulty was in establishing agreements on shipping. First we were sending the bananas with Maersk, the biggest container line shipper in the world. But when

Maersk changed their routing several containers missed their connections and arrived too late, with considerable damage to the fruit as a result. Attempts to work with T-Port again failed because no permanent space on their ship could be secured. As a result AgroFair were forced to fill in the supply to the Swiss market with bananas from Costa Rica.

We decided to approach the biggest export company in Ecuador. Noboa is the fifth-largest banana company in the world and owns a fleet of banana ships, the Ecuadorian Line. The wealthy owner, Alvara Noboa, was also a populist politician who was trying to become the next president of Ecuador. Initially, the idea of selling shipping space to a bunch of small producers was not received well. There were concerns about our ability to guarantee deliveries and payments. But I struck up a good relationship with Fransisco Aguirre, an Ecuadorian American who was the commercial director of the shipping operation. It turned out that we both had a keen interest in rowing, an unusual sport in Ecuador, and we went rowing together on the river Guayas. A good personal relationship facilitated a good business relationship. For several months El Guabo had stable access to the best possible connection from Ecuador to Europe. It was working well but a major change within Noboa resulted in their banana division wanting to use all the space on its ships for their own bananas. Despite Fransisco's best efforts on our behalf, we were kicked off the ships. This was critical. Consistent access to shipping was going to either make or break El Guabo.

In the meantime, we had been making great efforts to improve our quality. Several farmers dropped out because they were not able or willing to comply with the strict criteria. This was unfortunate but it was essential that we set a high standard in order to ensure that AgroFair and the European retailers were happy with the quality of the bananas. And this policy yielded a dividend when, in the millennium year, AgroFair came up with a plan for a shipping contract of 20,000 boxes a week – more than four times what we had been shipping previously.

It was quite a risk to sign such a large contract, but the quantity involved, and the relationship with AgroFair, would give us the opportunity to resolve our shipping issues. It was probably going to be our only chance of establishing a stable logistic connection with Europe. So Jorge Ramirez and I decided to go for it. But progress was far from simple. The market conditions in Europe were depressed and AgroFair only managed to sell around 5,000 boxes of Fairtrade bananas a week; the rest had to be sold as conventional bananas, mostly into Eastern Europe, at a much lower price.[5]

The space in the ship had to be filled in order to avoid 'dead freight'. El Guabo was forced to reduce the prices paid to the producers. Each farmer was obliged to supply bananas for the conventional market as well as Fairtrade bananas at the normal guaranteed price. The higher margins made on the Fairtrade bananas were used to compensate for the losses on low priced conventional bananas. This was a tough sell to the farmers. On average they were hardly better off than selling their bananas to any other company. But Jorge, a farmer himself, had the charisma to convince the other farmers to stay loyal to their own cooperative. And, during the course of the year, the farmers were rewarded for their loyalty. The Fairtrade volumes started to grow, mainly because of increasing volumes in the Swiss market. The conventional volumes started to decrease, so that it became a healthier mix for El Guabo.

El Guabo also started to expand as many of the farmers from other villages, who had been part of the original Fairtrade plan, joined the cooperative. There are now 16 subgroups of farmers from El Guabo, all having a legal status and managing their own projects, and benefiting from Fairtrade prices and the Fairtrade premium.

In 1999 El Guabo also became a co-owner of AgroFair. Together with Coopetrabasur (Costa Rica) and Volta River Estates (Ghana) an international cooperative was formed: the Cooperative Producers of AgroFair (CPAF). During a meeting at the offices of Solidaridad this new cooperative became the owner of 50 per cent of the shares of AgroFair Europe; making AgroFair's concept of 'fair price, fair say and fair share' a workable reality. (Solidaridad owned the other 50 per cent of the shares). Jorge Ramirez became a board member of AgroFair, and Nico Roozen the chairman.

AGROFAIR

In 2001 I returned to the Netherlands to join AgroFair. It was a difficult time as the company turned out to be on the edge of collapse. There was insufficient liquidity, bills that could not be paid, an extremely low solvency and banks were nervous that they would lose the money they had lent to the company. The former director had left the company, taking a number of employees with him, and therefore there was hardly any institutional memory. It took about a year before the situation was stabilised.

In 2001 the European Union changed its banana import regime. Once again banana imports from South America were disadvantaged. Under the new scheme companies had to demonstrate proof of the previous value of their banana imports and the European Union published the regulation just six working days before a deadline was to be applied. In just six days AgroFair had to form three new legal entities, with around 32 participating companies, and organise an auditors declaration in order to prove that minimum import values had been realised. In addition, a bank guarantee for €120 million had to be presented in order for our application to be considered. This was outrageous for a company which, at that time, had an annual turnover of only €20 million. Working day and night we somehow managed to get it done. We managed to secure access to the market for years to come but at considerable cost. In contrast, most of the traditional banana companies had secured most of their import quota for free.

Nevertheless, AgroFair was able to increase its volumes during the first decade of the new millennium. Having established a foothold in the Dutch, Belgian and Swiss markets the company started to explore the opportunities for Fairtrade a little further afield. The main target was the UK. In Britain the Co-op was showing serious interest in Fairtrade. At the same time we started speaking to Twin, who had introduced Cafédirect, a Fairtrade coffee brand. Together with Twin we established AgroFair UK to develop the market and, in conjunction with the Co-op, we introduced Fairtrade bananas to the UK.

A similar process took place in Italy, in partnership with CTM, an Italian Fairtrade organisation who were able to establish Fairtrade banana sales with Esselunga.[6] In Finland an unprecedented meeting of the three leading retailers resulted in an agreement to simultaneously introduce OKE bananas; with the support of the Finnish Fairtrade organisation volume increased rapidly to 15 per cent of the market. However, the biggest growth for AgroFair came from Switzerland where, in 2004, the Co-op became the first retailer in the world to switch all of its bananas to Fairtrade. This Swiss decision also resulted in a major growth opportunity for El Guabo who supplied the biggest chunk of the volume.

JORGE RAMIREZ

Jorge Ramirez played a major role in the successful development of both El Guabo and AgroFair. He was not only to gain the confidence of farmers, but also of retailers. He regularly met with retailers to offer the producers' perspective and was also a speaker at numerous events. When Agrofair introduced Fairtrade bananas to the Austrian market Jorge spoke directly to the Austrian parliament as part of the events organised to support the launch.

Although El Guabo had grown considerably he never ceased to worry about its future. It had never been set up to be a direct exporter but had become one out of necessity and he was worried about the difficulties of the combined roles of organisational politics and business administration which had evolved as a natural consequence of the direction the company had been forced to take. Jorge developed a plan in which a new export company was going to be established, which would be owned by the farmers, but which had external people in its governance structure. But Jorge became ill. He went to the local hospital for the treatment of what they thought was appendicitis. It turned out to be an aggressive cancer. There is a high incidence of cancer in banana regions which many believe is related to the use of agrochemicals. Whether or not Jorge's cancer was related to this we will never know. He went to Quito for further treatment, but the cancer was too far developed.

I flew to Quito to say goodbye. That same weekend a busload of producers and employees from El Guabo travelled to Quito to visit him. It was an emotional gathering. His brother asked him where he wanted to be buried, in Quito or El Guabo. Jorge did not hesitate for a second. He wanted to be buried in El Guabo. A few days after I left Quito, Jorge died. He was brought to El Guabo where a *velorio* (funeral wake) was organised. An enormous number of people came to say goodbye. He was buried in the local cemetery of El Guabo. A statue of him was made and placed in one of the rural communities that form a part of the El Guabo cooperative.

NOTES

1. El Niño is a climate pattern that occurs across the Pacific Ocean on average every five years. The event is usually associated with floods and other adverse weather conditions. The event of 1998 was particularly severe.
2. Exporters make forward commitments on shipping in order to guarantee space on the ships for their fruit. If the quantity falls short of their commitment they are still liable for the shipping charge. This is known as 'dead freight'.
3. Peter Chapman, *Bananas: How the United Fruit Company Shaped the World*, Canongate, 2007, pp. 70–4, 123–6.
4. Banana Link, www.bananalink.org.uk/content/view/66/26/lang,en/
5. The term 'conventional bananas' is simply used to describe bananas which are not Fairtrade.
6. CTM Altromercato is Italy's largest alternative trading organisation; it includes 118 organisations (associations and cooperatives) which are responsible for the management of 230 World Shops throughout Italy. Esselunga is an Italian retail chain which holds about 9 per cent of the grocery market.

Part II

Consumers

6
Campaigning for Justice

Joe Human and Bruce Crowther

THE GARSTANG STORY

Fairtrade has been a grassroots revolution. Just a few thousand committed, dedicated and like-minded individuals changed the attitudes of a nation and inspired a worldwide movement. By the time you read this there will be over 1,000 Fairtrade Towns[1] worldwide, including the cities of London, Paris, Rome, Brussels, Copenhagen, Wellington and San Francisco. The Fairtrade Town movement has the potential to create the largest single global campaign network ever seen and it all started in the very ordinary, traditional Lancashire market town of Garstang, with a population of just over 5,000. Fairtrade Towns are not about special people in special places but about ordinary people in ordinary places doing very special things.

It was the Garstang Oxfam Group which was responsible for making Garstang the world's first Fairtrade Town. Over the years, taking its mandate from Oxfam, the group had focused on many issues relating to global poverty, including trade issues. But following the introduction of the FAIRTRADE Mark into the UK in 1994 the promotion of Fairtrade became a particular favourite for two reasons. First, they argued, the concept of 'fair trade' should be a very easy message to understand: no hand outs, please, simply the right of producers to earn a 'fair day's pay for a fair day's work'. ('Justice not charity' was a message to which people in the 'industrial' North of England should be able to relate quite easily.) Second, once people understood the message, it would be very easy for them to take positive and effective action: all they had to do was to change the brand of their basic consumables, tea, coffee or chocolate. What could be simpler?

However, it wasn't quite so simple. The spectacles through which trade justice campaigners look at the world are not the same as most other people's, and Garstang's campaigners had very little success initially in reaching out into the community. Their letters to the local press on issues of international development could not compete with local concerns. And their pleas to the Town Council to use Fairtrade tea and coffee at their meetings were rebuffed with the illogical response that the councillors did not drink enough to make it worthwhile! It was even a struggle with faith groups. When six local churches were given catering packs of Fairtrade Cafédirect coffee in an attempt to get them to switch permanently to Fairtrade products, only half of them obliged. This was almost, but not quite, the final blow. If churches wouldn't change, who would?

Here it is important to emphasise that what is now a global movement started with years of intense frustration, through the failure of a very simple and obvious idea to catch on. But with the benefit of hindsight we can see that the campaigners' subsequent breakthrough is now one of the movement's greatest strengths: for if failure could eventually be turned into success in Garstang it could happen anywhere.

So what was the breakthrough? And this is the wonderful part of the story: the Group would not give up. In Fairtrade Fortnight 2000 they invited representatives of different sections of the community to a meal of Fairtrade and local produce. Local produce was used alongside Fairtrade because for campaigners in rural Garstang it was vital to show empathy with local farmers who also struggle to get a fair price for their produce.[2] Guests were not asked to pay for the meal, or even to make a donation. Instead they were asked to sign a form pledging to sell Fairtrade products, or when this was not possible, to use them on their premises.

From this well-attended event progress took a little time, but eventually the council, all the churches and schools, and 95 per cent of all the small businesses in the town signed the pledge. At the annual Public Meeting that followed, the people of Garstang voted to make Garstang a 'Fairtrade Town'. George Foulkes MP (then the Under Secretary of State for the Department for International Development), visiting Garstang later that year to congratulate them, said, 'The beacon that has started in Garstang can spread like wildfire through the whole country and beyond.'

From the start Garstang's determined campaigners recognised the FAIRTRADE Mark as the best vehicle for bringing the alternative fair trading system into the mainstream. Therefore, their campaign, and the Fairtrade Towns Initiative which followed, focused on promoting awareness and recognition of the FAIRTRADE Mark. The greater the sales of products bearing the mark, the greater the potential impact on the livelihoods of producers.

Their persistence paid off. A survey in 2001 showed that 71 per cent of local people recognised the FAIRTRADE Mark compared to a national average at that time of only 20 per cent. This success, however, would have very little impact on the lives of producers unless it could be replicated in the way that George Foulkes had predicted by 'spread[ing] like wildfire through the whole country and beyond'. So in 2001 the Fairtrade Foundation developed the framework of five goals as the basis for becoming a Fairtrade Town, City, Village, Island, Borough, County or Zone, which, for simplicity, are collectively referred to as 'Fairtrade Towns'.

These five goals were based on the success of the Garstang campaign[3] in involving the whole community, but had to be flexible enough to be applied to any size of place, from Fair Isle with a population of just 65 to London with a population of 7 million.

The five goals used in the UK[4] are as follows:

1. Local council passes a resolution supporting Fairtrade, and agrees to serve Fairtrade coffee and tea at its meetings and in its offices and canteens.
2. A range of Fairtrade products are readily available to buy in the area's shops and in local cafés/catering establishments (targets are set in relation to the population size of the area concerned).
3. Fairtrade products are used by a number of local work places and community organisations (faith groups, schools etc).
4. The campaign must attract media coverage and popular support.
5. A local Fairtrade steering group is convened to ensure continued commitment to its Fairtrade Town status.

HOW THE FAIRTRADE RIPPLES SPREAD, 2000–10

From the beginning the idea of making your community into a 'Fairtrade Town' captured the imagination and enthusiasm not only of trade justice campaigners, but also many tens of thousands more for whom the principle of 'fair dealing' is a part of the way they want to live. Thus even before Garstang was officially awarded Fairtrade Town status in November 2001, their self-declaration in April 2000 attracted the attention of local, regional, national and international media, and through them the notice of sharp-eyed campaigners elsewhere. The first of these was Linda Fabiani MSP,[5] who decided to make her constituency town, Strathaven in Scotland, a Fairtrade Town.

Within a short time campaigners up and down the land were racing to make their communities into the 'firsts' – the first in their region, county or country with Fairtrade 'status', be it town, city, village, island, borough or county. Yet others competed to make 'Fairtrade firsts' of completely different sorts: the first valley, the first district, the first national park, or even the 'highest', the 'lowest', the 'smallest', etc. To help bring a semblance of order to what threatened to be an unmanageable proliferation, the Fairtrade Foundation created the category of 'Fairtrade Zone' to cover *all* places outside one of the other six categories (of Town, City, Village, Island, Borough, County).

However, before very long creative campaigners began to recognise yet more 'entities' – *within* their communities: 'Fairtrade schools' and 'Fairtrade churches', and then any organisation or business which supported Fairtrade: 'Fairtrade railways', 'Fairtrade airports', 'Fairtrade hospitals' and even 'Fairtrade prisons'! Again, grassroots campaigners were ahead of the Foundation, who in response developed yet more categories.

At present in the UK, there are Fairtrade Churches, Dioceses (and other denominational groups), Synagogues, Mosques, Hindu Temples, Sikh gurdwara, Bahai places of worship, Universities and Schools,[6] all officially recognised by the Fairtrade Foundation. And although there is some pressure to expand the list further; campaigners recognise the need for a limit, to prevent the system becoming unwieldy and losing its integrity as a community-based movement.

The first development beyond the UK came in 2003, when Fairtrade Ireland developed their own Fairtrade Town initiative using the five UK goals, but adding a sixth requiring the participation of schools. Clonakilty became the first Irish Fairtrade Town, based on the six criteria. Two years later Belgium started a Fairtrade Towns campaign, also adding a sixth goal: support for local produce. Following the Fair Trade Futures conference in Chicago in 2005 and together with the labelling organisation TransFair USA,[7] American Alternative Trading Organizations explored ways to start a Fair Trade Towns initiative in the US. In 2006 fair trade supporters in Media, Pennsylvania, inspired by the pioneering work they had seen in Garstang, declared their community the first Fair Trade Town in the US, on the basis of the UK criteria. This kick-started the Fair Trade Towns campaign in the US which now not only promotes fair trade, but includes other alternative fair trading systems.

The Wales Fair Trade Forum, likewise supporting both the FAIRTRADE Mark and other fair trade systems, developed their own criteria for a 'Fair Trade Nation' (two words!). Building on the achievements of many Welsh Fairtrade

Towns, Counties, Schools and Churches, the Forum declared Wales the world's first Fair Trade Nation in 2008. Scotland, with a similar campaign, may well have declared by the time you read this.

Until 2008 the Fairtrade Towns movement had been confined to the countries of the global north, specifically those with Labelling Initiatives,[8] e.g. the Fairtrade Foundation in the UK and Max Havelaar in the Netherlands. But in December 2008 coffee producers in Alfenas declared their community the first 'Fair Trade Town' in Brazil, and a year later Pérez Zeledón in Costa Rica followed suit. With these declarations in countries in the south, where there is no Fairtrade label (or Labelling Initiative), but where there are Fairtrade *producers*, a completely new dimension was introduced into the movement. This challenged 'northern' exclusivity of the awards system, and opened a new chapter in the unfolding story of the Fairtrade Towns movement.

By mid 2010, 16 of the 19 Fairtrade Labelling Initiatives were involved with Fairtrade Town initiatives: UK, Ireland, Belgium, France, Germany, Austria, the Netherlands, Italy, Spain, Denmark, Norway, Sweden, Finland, the US, Canada, and Australia and New Zealand (covered by a single labelling organisation).

In July 2009 the International Fairtrade Towns website[9] was launched with its own social forum. The site provides an important tool for sharing learning and facilitating greater communication across the global movement, not only for national coordinators and local campaigners, but also for other trade justice activists. In most participating countries, informal networks are now developing, and in one or two places are well developed.[10] National campaigns have worked jointly on international events such as World Fair Trade Day[11] and have competed to set world coffee drinking and banana eating records. There has also been some coordination on Fairtrade Fortnight.

The graph in Figure 6.1 shows the growth of Fairtrade Towns within Britain, a growth marked by a slow start, a rapid rise between 2004 and 2008, and a slight slackening of the rate of growth since then.

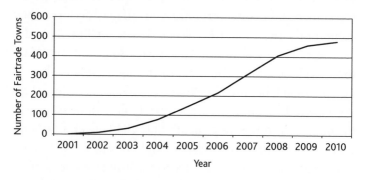

Figure 6.1   Growth of Fairtrade Towns in the UK
Total up to April 2010 = 479

The international situation is shown in the second graph, Figure 6.2, with starting dates for each country in brackets. The graph includes Brazil and Costa Rica, where as yet there are no Labelling Initiatives. Relative to the sizes of their populations Ireland, Belgium, and Austria have done remarkably, while others still have 'much potential'.[12] Japan, which does not feature in the graph, launched its Fairtrade Towns campaign in March 2010. In the pipeline are Fairtrade Towns campaigns in the Czech Republic, Ghana, Nigeria and Poland.

Looking back at the story of Garstang and the ripples which have spread out from it, it can be seen that the

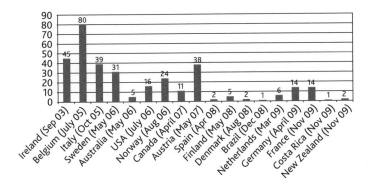

Figure 6.2 Numbers of Fair Trade Towns outside the UK
Total up to April 2010 = 336

turning point for the Oxfam Group in the transition from failure to success came when they (self-)declared Garstang a 'Fairtrade Town'. This success arising from their initial failure has been not just an example but an inspiration to countless others. One could say that the difficult birth in Garstang has enabled others to conceive. There was and still is nothing special about Garstang. And it is that very ordinariness, that nothing-specialness, which sends out the clear and inspiring message to all: that wherever there is a will and a commitment, *any* community can achieve what Garstang achieved and become a Fairtrade Town – *anywhere* in the world.

WHY HAS THE MOVEMENT BEEN SO SUCCESSFUL?

Campaigners are given to (and can be forgiven for!) the occasional hyperbole, but it is no exaggeration to say that the Fairtrade Towns movement is one of the most extraordinary grassroots consumer movements ever: extraordinary both in terms of the dynamism of its growth and, now, in its global reach. What has made it so?

Fairtrade itself is such a simple idea. The notion – the principle – of paying a 'fair price' and a 'fair wage', especially to people who produce our food, who work hard in so doing but stay poor, is embedded within the ethical framework of most people. And while people like a bargain, and while many have little choice but to shop for 'value', at the same time most are repulsed by the idea of exploitation. Fairtrade simply chimes with our notions of basic human decency, to whichever culture we belong.[13]

The notion of a 'fair price' and a 'fair wage', of course, is not new, certainly not in Britain. The cooperative movement was founded on the principle that neither producers nor consumers should be cheated and that both should be treated fairly. But until quite recently the application of the principle rarely extended to producers or consumers beyond our horizons. However, in the last 30 years our horizons have widened beyond imagination, through travel, global migration, the print and broadcast media, and most recently through the web. All of which have led to unprecedented levels of consumer awareness and the growth of 'ethical' consumerism.

We now know so much more, about people in other places, the lives they lead, and their aspirations. We also know so much more about how, in a globalised world, they connect with us, and about the real and potential impact which we may have on them, and they on us. Moreover we know, and generally care, much more about where and how our food is produced, about the people who produce it, and about the broader issues and injustices of global trade.

There is, too, a growing distaste for and resentment of the power of the 'big players' (multinational corporations, supermarkets, etc). While this has focused in particular on the treatment of our own farmers, with respect, for example, to milk and fresh vegetables and fruit, there has been growing concern about similar abuses with respect to overseas producers, particularly small scale farmers. Arising from this there is an increasing desire to hold the 'big boys', most especially the supermarkets, to account, a concern which now connects to the issues of climate change and sustainability.[14]

For more and more people simply to know the facts, and to be concerned about them, is not enough – they need to act. While many committed individuals have been taking action for years, marching with the Jubilee Debt campaign, Making Poverty History, lobbying their MPs on trade justice, and so on, all would acknowledge that lobbying is hard work. It is also time consuming, and its positive outcomes, though always welcome, are all too rare. On the other hand shopping Fairtrade works *every* time. You can do it every day, and every time you do, you *know* it makes a difference. As a result of your conscious choice to buy this (Fairtrade) coffee rather than that (non-Fairtrade) brand, people in some distant place, whom you will never meet, will get a guaranteed fair price for the product and a fair wage for their labour. This *is* hugely empowering for many people – people who may never have seen themselves as activists, who may never have written a lobbying letter, met their MPs or gone on marches, but people who want to shop with a better conscience, and can now do so.[15] Fairtrade simply becomes their way of doing 'trade justice' *at the check-out*.

In this way Fairtrade not only connects with people's personal 'values', whether faith-based or secular-humanist, capitalist or socialist: it also provides them with the opportunity to align their spending with their principles, and feel good about it. Even anti-capitalists shop and anti-globalisers drink coffee!

But there is even more to it. For each act of 'revolution' at the check-out sends a signal to business, government and society about how people want trade to work. Each purchase is a vote for a different way of doing trade, one that puts people at the heart.

While Fairtrade campaigners come from all classes and income groups, and from almost all political parties, and span both generations and genders, the commitment of the churches, and more recently of other religious denominations, in translating 'faith' into action has played a significant part in energising the grassroots movement. In most communities there will have been at least one church whose members will have seen that the imperative of the gospel translates for them into actions for social justice, of which Fairtrade will naturally be one strand, along with charitable giving. And through the growth of ecumenism and local 'Churches Together' alliances, the message of engagement has spread from church to church. Most church communities will for years have had strong connections to faith-based NGOs, such as CAFOD, Christian Aid and Tearfund. Some, too, may have sold Fairtrade and fairly traded products from Traidcraft stalls at the back of the church.

It is hardly surprising that in the movement's short history, a significant number of Fairtrade campaign groups have developed within church communities, and while some still are rooted within churches, it has made good sense to many to break away to reach out to non-confessional constituencies, particularly in culturally diverse communities.

What amazes many campaigners is the slowness and indifference of some church communities, and even the hostility of others, to engage with Fairtrade. On the other hand the more recent engagement of other faiths has been greatly welcomed, demonstrating again the fact that Fairtrade reaches across communities within the context of wide social and cultural diversities.

In addition to the role played by the confessional agencies, such as Christian Aid, that of the secular agencies has been very influential. Both Oxfam and the World Development Movement (WDM) have extensive networks of activists and campaigning groups, who, particularly in the early years, were the drivers of local campaigns. To these can be added the secular National Federation of Women's Institutes (NFWI)[16] and Soroptimist International, both of which provide very large constituencies of support nationwide.

The advantage of secular campaign networks is that they have no perceived allegiances to other constituencies, and have, therefore, potentially a wider reach. However, in the end, the combined contribution of all of these agencies – confessional and secular – has been greater than the sum of the parts. Indeed the success of the grassroots movement is in no small way the result of its appeal across almost all constituencies. Fairtrade is inclusive and connecting – we can *all* do it. Furthermore, if a community decides to go for Fairtrade status, the five goals make that a necessity, and for that endeavour the FAIRTRADE Mark itself provides a unity of purpose.

Paralleling the growth of Fairtrade activism within communities and churches has been the growth of awareness and activism within schools. In some schools, Fairtrade has been driven by students themselves, supported by world-aware teachers. Elsewhere it has been the other way round. Everywhere the implications of, and the opportunities presented by, curricula of both global citizenship and moral education have provided the educational context for translating learning into *active* citizenship: not just understanding, but doing.

Many young campaigners have taken the cause with them into their higher education. At the time of writing, there are now almost 120 Fairtrade Universities in Britain, within which cafeterias and refectories, coffee shops and bars, have Fairtrade products available to all students – and that will include those who have not come from Fairtrade schools or Fairtrade committed families. And whatever they may, or may not do, by way of campaigning when they graduate, most will continue to be Fairtrade consumers.

None of this nationwide activism could have happened without two other elements: first, the energy, commitment, skills and imagination of grassroots campaigners, and second the multiple roles played by the Fairtrade Foundation in supporting the movement.

The sheer exuberance and abundance of campaigners' ideas; the range of their talents and experiences (many have lived and worked overseas in development); the genius of their publicity stunts, and skilled use of local media; their clever identification of key 'multipliers' and their effective targeting of influential 'levers'; their creative alliance building[17] and deft networking (learning from, competing with and inspiring each other);[18] their ability to make small resources go a long way; their talent for galvanising public support for the cause, especially to win over resistant councils; their refusal to let disappointments deter them and their joyous celebration of every success – all these have contributed to the seemingly inexhaustible energy of local campaigns.

Even the most committed campaigners, however, need returns, and in the last few years these have been abundant too. For almost all of them, the journey of Fairtrade products from the margins to the mainstream, from Oxfam shelves and stalls at the back of churches to supermarket aisles, has been a massive and visible sign of their success. After years of dismissing Fairtrade, and a few more of resisting it, most 'big players' are now seriously engaged. Paradoxically this is not entirely to the liking of some activists who have always been suspicious of supermarkets' motives. But Fairtrade operates within a free trade context: no-one has to shop in Tesco if they don't like it.

In terms of both leadership and support for campaigners, the Fairtrade Foundation has played a key role, coming up with ever more brilliant ideas, and imaginative resources, including an excellent website. Their support is seen at its best in the run up to and during the annual themed Fairtrade Fortnight in February/March. The Foundation's investment in bringing Fairtrade producers to Britain to talk about the transforming power of Fairtrade on their lives is worth a thousand leaflets. To have a banana farmer speaking in a village hall or at a primary school assembly, or a coffee farmer on a university campus or in a council chamber can have more impact in one hour than years of doorstep campaigning.[19] And to the power of producers' stories can be added those of the many committed 'celebrities', who have seen Fairtrade in action for themselves.

As the Foundation has scaled up, their support has got better and better. Furthermore, with the weight of the movement behind it the success of the Foundation in securing the engagement of the big players has given campaigners the returns they need to keep going. It has been a truly virtuous circle.

Within this story of success we have identified a number of key players: church communities and other faith constituencies; major development organisations, e.g. Oxfam, Christian Aid, WDM and CAFOD and their grassroots supporters; Traidcraft which has been at the forefront of product development (getting fairly traded products Fairtrade branded) and which has its own network of Fair Traders; secular national movements, particularly the NFWI and Soroptimist International; and the Fairtrade Foundation itself.

Over and above all of these, however, has been the boundless energy and creative imagination of grassroots activists and campaigning groups, in their villages and towns, their schools and colleges, who have driven the campaign at the local level; who have known how to ask the right questions of the right people; and how to persuade and to secure changes in attitudes and practice in businesses and faith groups, workplaces and households. In short – to paraphrase the words of self-help manuals – how to make Fairtrade friends and influence people.

NOTES

1. The use of the terms 'Fairtrade' and 'Fair Trade' causes much confusion for the public and even for campaigners. In the UK and many other European countries all products bearing the FAIRTRADE Mark and meeting international Fairtrade standards set and monitored by Fairtrade Labelling Organizations International (FLO) are referred to as 'Fairtrade' (one word), as are those towns, cities, villages, etc. awarded status by the national Fairtrade Labelling Initiative (which in the case of the UK is the

Fairtrade Foundation). In Germany, the US and Canada, however, products branded with the Mark, and communities which have received status, are 'Fair Trade' (two words). Further confusion is caused by the fact that TransFair Canada and USA (their equivalents of the Fairtrade Foundation) use a different mark altogether. For simplicity, in this chapter we shall use the term 'Fairtrade Towns'.

2. Fairtrade campaigners have continued to draw the parallels between Fairtrade and local, particularly in areas where farming is a challenge for both environmental and economic reasons.

3. For more on Garstang visit www.garstangfairtrade.org.uk

4. For full details see www.fairtrade.org.uk/get_involved/campaigns/fairtrade_towns/the_5_goals.aspx

5. Member of the Scottish Parliament.

6. There are now over 6,000 churches, 78 dioceses and other denominational groups, 39 synagogues, 1 mosque, and 1 Hindu temple, 1 Sikh gurdwara, 1 Bahai place of worship, 350 schools (with over a further 4,000 registered), and 119 universities with Fairtrade status.

7. The US equivalent of the Fairtrade Foundation.

8. Fairtrade Labelling Initiatives (sometimes referred to as 'labelling organisations') license the FAIRTRADE Mark on products and promote Fairtrade in their territory. As founding members, many of these organisations helped to establish the Bonn-based Fairtrade Labelling Organization International in 1997. There are 19 Labelling Initiatives covering 23 countries.

9. www.fairtradetowns.org

10. For example, in Cumbria, UK (www.cumbriafairtrade.org.uk).

11. World Fair Trade Day, which takes place on the second Saturday in May, is an initiative of the World Fair Trade Organization (WFTO, www.wfto.com). The World Fair Trade Organization is the global network of Fair Trade Organizations around the world. It represents more than 350 Fair Trade Organizations from more than 70 countries.

12. There is broad correlation between the number of Fairtrade Towns and the per capita annual expenditure on Fairtrade.

13. Although it is often said that fairness is a particularly British trait, there are probably no cultures in which principles of equity are entirely absent.

14. For early Fairtrade activists Fairtrade was simply an extension of their campaigning on trade justice, and for many groups Fairtrade is still located within that context. But increasingly campaigners see Fairtrade's links to issues of sustainability, to shopping locally for local products, and to the issues of climate change and 'climate justice'.

15. While Fairtrade is usually framed in terms of 'empowerment through trade' (for producers and workers in developing countries), the parallel for campaigners and consumers in developing countries is rarely acknowledged. For many consumers – and campaigners too – Fairtrade can be transformational in the way they see and relate to the world.

16. Founder members of the Fairtrade Foundation were CAFOD, Christian Aid, Oxfam, Traidcraft and WDM. Member organisations now also include Banana Link, Methodist Relief and Development Fund, Nicaragua Solidarity Campaign, People and Planet, SCIAF, Shared Interest, Soroptimist International, Tearfund and the United Reformed Church. Though not a founder member of the Fairtrade Foundation, the NFWI have been involved in its governance since almost the beginning.

17. Many Fairtrade groups have built very effective links with local sustainability campaigns. In some communities Fairtrade is 'located' within the context of campaigning on local sustainability as part of the Transition Towns movement.

18. Many national campaigns have developed their own on-line discussion groups. There is also an international Fairtrade Towns discussion group.

19. For a small number of Fairtrade local campaigns the power of the personal witness of visiting Fairtrade farmers has been greatly strengthened through links between the group and a Fairtrade producer community. As examples, we cite Garstang's link with New Korofidua, Ghana (www.garstangfairtrade.org.uk/ghana/index.html) and Keswick's with Choche, Ethiopia (www.fairtrade-keswick.org.uk/?c=ethiopia&a=index).

7

A Glass and a Half Full –
How Cadbury Embraced Fairtrade

David Croft and Alex Cole

INTRODUCTION

When Cadbury announced that Britain's most popular chocolate bar, Dairy Milk, was going Fairtrade in March 2009, many consumers wondered why it had taken so long. Yet those in the know wondered how it could be possible at all, given the move would more than double the amount of cocoa bought under the sustainable farming scheme. Could Fairtrade farmers supply such a massive increase in such a short time? And what impact would this have on the rest of the mainstream chocolate market?

The detail behind the headlines reveals a complex recipe of business realities, corporate values and heritage and a commercial opportunity. And in typically 'glass-and-a-half' fashion, Cadbury was also aiming to bring something to the Fairtrade party, rather than taking a free-ride on the movement.

For nearly 200 years Cadbury had been at the vanguard of corporate social responsibility, yet its very success and modern-day scale meant that adopting a certification scheme like Fairtrade seemed impossible. Whilst Fairtrade was rapidly growing in prominence, its formula seemed firmly fixed on small, niche ethical brands, squarely targeted at ethical consumers who would be willing to pay premium prices for premium brands. Green & Black's – a pioneer of Fairtrade and one of the first products to be certified back in 1994 – perfectly exemplified this. Its Maya Gold bar supported the brand's positioning as the UK's favourite organic chocolate, happily ensconced at the top end of the market with a price to match. However, acquired by Cadbury in 2005, it brought ethical sourcing know-how into the organisation, and Fairtrade Cadbury another step closer.

Cadbury, with a far broader consumer base, needed first and foremost to address the primary concerns of UK chocolate lovers – taste and value – as well as the practical constraints of volume. So it was with these non-negotiables in mind that a small team inside Cadbury planned to add values into the mix and give the Fairtrade movement a timely boost along the way.

In many ways, the time was ripe for a big brand to take this significant step forward. All the supermarkets were exploring Fairtrade's fit within their supply chain, including parts of their own-label chocolate production. Awareness levels of Fairtrade had never been higher, aided in particular by the growth of Fairtrade in the 'out-of-home' trade in tea and coffee, but also by the movement's work through schools and churches. Chocolate, as one of the nation's favourite affordable luxuries, would be the perfect poster child for a new breed of Fairtrade – tipping the balance to take it into every corner shop and home across the country.

The team at Cadbury saw the chance to turn a number of issues into the opportunity to take that step:

- Consumers, major chocolate brands and cocoa processors such as Cargill and Barry Callebaut, had growing concerns about labour standards and the use of child labour in West Africa. While Fairtrade was not a guarantee, its audit and certification process as well as community development were seen as part of the solution by many, including international Non-Governmental Organisations (NGOs) and the American political lobby.

- Supply of cocoa was failing to match the increase in demand, particularly in Cadbury's case in Ghana. A combination of an ageing farmer population and outdated farming methods was a recipe for an industry in decline and lower than average productivity levels.

It was this second issue of supply which lay at the heart of Cadbury's move, with the foundations laid through the creation of a unique Cadbury Cocoa Partnership. Todd Stitzer, Cadbury's chief executive until April 2010, described this: 'Lots of people think that the Fairtrade is all about reputation, marketing and the brand – about getting an ethical "badge". But it's much more fundamental. It's about supply chain sustainability.'[1] Cadbury realised they needed to be much more active right across the economic, social and environmental aspects of cocoa farmers' lives for the good of their own business.

But the organisation of the complex and massive cocoa supply chain, with its hundreds of thousands of small farmers, was seen as a fundamental barrier to certification. Ghana, Cadbury's main source of cocoa, has over 700,000 cocoa farmers, each typically working a tiny farm of two to three hectares.[2] Côte d'Ivoire has almost twice that number. These are simple farms, usually informally set up with cocoa trees growing under the shade of other forest trees often without the regimen that consumers in the UK would associate with massive farming operations.

Manufacturers and processors typically have limited direct contact with these farmers. In the case of Ghana, cocoa is bought through the Ghanaian government's Cocobod organisation, a semi-liberalised system that trades Ghanaian cocoa on the world market. This system has the advantage of setting an annual price so farmers know in advance what they will get paid for each 65kg sack of dried cocoa beans they harvest, helping them plan their limited finances. Cocobod's systems also guarantee only high quality cocoa is traded internationally, enabling Ghana to command a price premium around 10 per cent above the world market. However, it makes direct dealings with farmers difficult, therefore making certifying specific farms and groups of farmers challenging. Côte d'Ivoire has a different approach without any government agencies, but it is complex for different reasons. A long series of middlemen bridge the trading relationships between farmers and exporters such that any work at farm level to enable certification requires significant resources. The complexities in both countries made large scale Fairtrade certification difficult. Cadbury and the other big global brands use tens of thousands of tonnes of cocoa each year compared with the 3,000 tonnes of Fairtrade cocoa traded from Ghana. To meet the needs of a brand the size of Cadbury Dairy Milk would pose its own challenge to the Fairtrade organisation.

At its heart Fairtrade isn't about marketing, despite what the UK consumer might believe. It's about people and communities who are at the heart of complex supply chains.

It's about how they link to a complex consumer marketplace in a distant part of the world. And it's about connections that go beyond simple ingredients to the organisational values that define both Cadbury and Fairtrade.

CADBURY AND FAIRTRADE – THE VALUES NEXUS

The history of Cadbury is one that is well known in the UK and is fundamental to the journey that led Cadbury Dairy Milk to become Fairtrade. When the Cadbury brothers built the now famous 'factory in the garden' in Bournville in 1879, they were one of a small group of philanthropic industrialists of their era, a group that also included the Lever Brothers at Port Sunlight that grew to the huge Unilever company of the twentieth century. They believed that business success and social values were linked, and the route to success. While today a whole industry of commentators and practitioners seek to identify a definitive link between Corporate Social Responsibility (CSR) and success in the marketplace, for the Cadbury family it was simple. Looking after the welfare of their factory staff meant a more effective workforce. The very basis of the original business in cocoa drinks was inspired in support of the temperance movement to bring the common man nourishment and a way to avoid the temptations of alcohol. This was supported by the family's Quaker roots which brought strong values into the business, from the positioning of Cadbury products to the way the company developed and ran its factory. They created housing and leisure facilities for their workforce and were one of the first companies to introduce pensions and paid leave.

These values were a driving force within the business, but the brothers were not just philanthropists. They were what Todd Stitzer has termed 'principled capitalists'. Ambitious, innovative and successful business people who made money and created a company that grew to become a world leader. Arguably, the Cadbury brothers in the nineteenth century forged a link between business growth and business values that modern researchers are still struggling to truly identify. At times that link clearly supported industrial success; in simple terms, a modern, supported, safe workforce was more productive. At other times, the Cadbury brothers saw the social imperative of the approach operating far beyond the confines of the factory walls, seeing business as a force for good and being an asset to the neighbourhood.

Of course the Cadbury family answered only to themselves. Today shareholders own the company and expect a return on their investment. Cadbury is now a global business, operating in over 200 countries and a world leader in confectionery. From a small shop in Birmingham in 1824, it has become first or second in the majority of confectionery markets across the globe and, in Cadbury chocolate and Trident gum, has two brands valued at more than $1 billion annually. Cadbury was, for a while, the largest confectionery business in the world until the merger of Mars Inc. and the Wrigley Corporation. With the acquisition of Cadbury by Kraft Foods in 2010, it is again the world's confectionery leader, within the broader Kraft Foods portfolio.

On the modern corporate stage, delivering superior shareholder value is non-negotiable and more than ever there is a need to demonstrate the value of values. Yet those nineteenth century Cadbury themes are clearly present in the twenty-first century business with the move to Fairtrade frequently cited as the exemplar of this approach. As Todd Stitzer says, 'We came to Fairtrade because of the value it can bring to our supply chain and because of our values. Said another way, quality cocoa for us and a better quality of life for thousands of farmers, empowered through Fairtrade to reinvest in their own farms and communities.'[3]

This was seen in the values of the business, which were in turn integrated into the core business strategy. Cadbury describes itself as a 'performance driven – values led' company.[4] Since 2006 a strong sustainability agenda has been delivered, built from the CSR foundation that had been formalised from 2000, all bearing the hallmarks of the original Cadbury brothers' formula.

Internally, management practice follows a series of business principles that all leaders sign each year, and which reinforce the core values of Performance, Quality, Integrity, Respect and Responsibility.[5] Externally, Cadbury has taken a lead on business sustainability with groundbreaking activity on the environmental agenda, being the first in the sector to make the leap to 'absolute' carbon emission targets, and developing sustainable agriculture including work on cocoa farming.[6]

These developments demonstrate a significant strategic evolution. In the past the approach may have been CSR-driven, or have a business benefit that may have derived from enlightened self-interest. Now it also embraces advocacy across the business and consumer spheres, creating a wider campaigning and public perspective that sets Cadbury apart from most other global multinational companies. This is coupled with a strong commercial focus that drives financial return from putting sustainability into a commercial context through products, supply chains and brands. Returning to Todd Stitzer's thoughts on principled capitalism 'where wisdom, judgement and perspective help to balance the positive focus on value creation that comes from a profit motive and delivery of shareholder value with wider values to deliver a more successful and sustainable business'.[7] Here the company is playing a role in society that is much broader than simple industrial output and wealth creation to shareholders, employees and suppliers. While it may not please followers of Adam Smith, it is very much aligned to the Cadbury brothers' ethos of business being a force for good, marking the twenty-first century update of their approach and a strategic transition from philanthropy through corporate responsibility to business sustainability.

These values within the Cadbury operating culture are similar to the values of the Fairtrade movement. Where Fairtrade talks about Transparency, Empowerment and Equity,[8] Cadbury promotes Respect and Responsibility.[9] And Cadbury chose to make their work on cocoa the embodiment of this. In a Board discussion on sustainability in 2006, it was noted that if saving the planet is the world's greatest challenge where Cadbury needed to play its part, then cocoa sustainability was the confectionery industry's greatest challenge and one which Cadbury needed to tackle head on.

NO BEANS, NO BARS – SECURING CADBURY'S SUPPLY OF COCOA

The rationale for more direct involvement in cocoa was, on the surface, pretty straightforward. Without the beans there would be no chocolate. Independent research commissioned by Cadbury revealed that while prices for cocoa are rising, some farmers are simply not producing enough to support their families and the next generation of farmers are moving away from the sector. Falling supplies against a backdrop of increasing demand is a recipe for an unsustainable business on all levels.

Whilst the average consumer may think that Cadbury chocolate comes from Bournville, its true source lies in the rainforests of Ghana. Cocoa's scientific name – *Theobroma cacao* – literally means 'Food of the Gods' and this magical ingredient is famed as the most complex food substance on earth (it contains over 300 identifiable compounds including an abundance of natural anti-stress, anti-depressant and bliss inducing compounds). Ghanaian cocoa has a particular flavour, a unique profile which makes Cadbury Dairy Milk taste like... well, like Cadbury.

Cadbury first began to develop cocoa sourcing in Ghana in 1908. Until this point, Cadbury's cocoa had come from the island of Sao Tome off the West Coast of Africa. However, investigations suggested that intertribal slavery might be in operation and led the Cadbury brothers to seek alternative sources that were in line with their value set. So they worked alongside farmers in the nearby Gold Coast, today's Ghana, to cultivate cocoa for the first time. As with Bournville, they invested in a range of community facilities and put in place many of the practices and frameworks which shaped Ghana's world leading cocoa sector. The first significant exports from Ghana to Cadbury came in 1909 and throughout the twentieth century the sector grew becoming Ghana's second biggest export, after gold.

As Cadbury sought to reconnect more directly with farmers, nearly a century later this history proved to be an invaluable asset. At its highpoint, Cadbury had nearly 1,000 personnel in Ghana. They had invested in education and community support through, for example, the Cadbury Hall at Ghana's Achimoto College where many Ghanaian leaders including President Atta-Mills have since studied. This history and these links provide an unrivalled connection to Ghana and its cocoa.

Of all the issues needing attention, cocoa supply was the most pressing from a business perspective. The level of productivity has grown little in recent years while demand has progressively increased, particularly with the emergence of chocolate lovers in developing markets. This was an issue which Cadbury was already working on, together with others in the industry, through the Sustainable Tree Crops Programme.[10] This was also supported by American government funding through USAID, and aimed to improve cocoa productivity through farmer training. However, with the numbers of cocoa farmers in West Africa totalling around 2 million, spread across several countries and frequently in remote rural communities, the Sustainable Tree Crops Programme faced serious challenges of scale.

Additionally, weakened productivity is not all down to farmer training. It is symptomatic of deeper issues within the West African cocoa sector. Ageing trees and a growing concern that soil health is deteriorating, compounding the problem and further reducing productivity.[11] The demographics of the farmer populations also tell their own story – typically farmers are over 50 years old, and the next generation are uninterested in becoming cocoa farmers and are drifting from rural communities to the growing urban centres.[12]

Separately, the challenge of tackling the worst forms of child labour in these same rural communities remains significant. The chocolate industry is working together with civil society partners to help tackle the issue through the International

Cocoa Initiative; however solving this complex issue requires a complex solution.[13] The initiative has developed community-based programmes to build awareness and solutions to child labour issues, working with West African governments to train enforcement agencies on trafficking and supporting rescue centres. These measures work best where the farming communities are also able to increase their economic strength and are part of wider development agendas, particularly in education and health.

All of these issues were the subject of a significant independent research by the Institute of Development Studies and the University of Ghana commissioned by Cadbury. This looked into the Ghanaian cocoa value chain to understand the pressures faced by farmers, their motivations and potential interventions to secure a sustainable cocoa future for both farmers and Cadbury.[14] The research engaged the Ghanaian cocoa sector at all levels, from farmers to government leaders. Workshops in Ghana helped create understanding of the challenges faced by farmers and helped to shape potential areas for intervention. It considered both typical farming practices, such as pest management and fertiliser use, and the socio-economic challenges in rural cocoa farming communities. It produced a holistic review of the cocoa value chain and identified some significant problems to be addressed.

In particular the importance of the community infrastructure was highlighted as a means of supporting sustainable cocoa farming activity for the future. Within Ghana, market access is not an issue for smallholder farmers, trading as they do through the nationalised sector. As a result, the role of farming communities or cooperatives is somewhat different from that needed elsewhere. However the value of the community was highlighted in terms of its potential to provide a vehicle for knowledge transfer through farmer training, and underpinning cooperative approaches to farming practice; and it was also perceived to have a key role in meeting the challenge of the worst forms of child labour, through sensitisation programmes and training for whole communities.

The research identified the crucial role of communities acting as a focus for rural development. This role has also been identified by the Ghanaian government in its own development programme that has aimed to set up rural enterprise units in each region.[15] However the scale of that activity is limited as Ghana invests in a wide range of development activities, and it is unlikely to materially affect the 700,000 or so cocoa farmers. As such, the development of communities that can define their own action plans for growth, empowerment, and development, remains important. In this sense, the link to the Fairtrade model and philosophy becomes increasingly apparent.

PARTNERSHIP IN COCOA

These issues were clearly beyond the remit of a simple confectionery company, even one with Cadbury's heritage. Development was not a core capability of the company best known for making Wispa bars and its award-winning 'drumming gorilla' TV commercial. So the first step was the formation of the Cadbury Cocoa Partnership in 2008, a coalition that works through a network of NGO partners and farming communities. With the aim of developing thriving rural communities that enable a sustainable cocoa supply chain, it is a unique, groundbreaking programme, investing £45 million over an initial ten year period.[16]

On the ground, activity in Ghana took the form of a long term development programme using the earlier research to set priorities and help find creative solutions. The strategic vision was underpinned by activity to support improved livelihoods from cocoa and other sectors for farming communities, broad community development and support for a policy framework that would enable cocoa farming communities to prosper. Ghana was just the start, with similar programmes in India and the Dominican Republic also commencing. The scale of the investment was unprecedented, the first of its kind from a multinational company in cocoa and indicating a desire to drive long term change and development at scale. The community-centric approach is reflected in the governance process for the Partnership, with international NGO representation on the global board and government, farmer, development and local NGO input in Ghana. Indeed, Kuapa Kokoo, the Fairtrade cooperative, is part of the board in Ghana.

The Partnership also marked a step-change in the prevailing business approach, shifting from a lack of engagement based on fear of scale or adverse reputational impact, to embracing the issues and recognising the benefits of active intervention rather than a passive response. There was also acceptance, based on widespread consultation and research, that the solution would lie in a development-driven, community-centric approach which required a different business approach and new working partners. The resulting Partnership and its investment plan was based upon a strong business case, supporting long term cocoa supply from a sustainable agricultural base whilst also tackling the socio-economic, environmental and reputational challenges that the cocoa sector was facing. As such, the Partnership was not a public relations exercise, but a development programme designed to support farmers, the cocoa supply chain and the Cadbury brand. It fundamentally fitted the original Cadbury brothers' ethos and the values of the company, and brought those values into a modern business context striking a balance across operational, reputational and commercial sectors.

Much in the Partnership's strategy resonates with Fairtrade. Both support poverty alleviation and sustainable development; both are producer-centric and aim to create opportunities for those producers disadvantaged or marginalised by prevailing trading systems.[17] These goals are underpinned by long term trading relationships helping to improve market access and which develop over time through mutual respect, transparency and commitment.

In terms of design and delivery, the activities of Fairtrade and Cadbury reflect a common value set. While their origins may be different – one based upon a desire to resolve social inequity, the other a business driven by values and enlightened self-interest – they had the potential to be natural partners. They share similar values and community-based approaches and, of course, Fairtrade producers were already engaged in the Partnership representing farmer interests.

The insurmountable challenge of the scale of supply required for Cadbury was also unlocked by the Partnership. Its advent created the scale of investment that would enable broader agricultural and community development, engagement with existing Fairtrade farming communities allowing them to grow further, and support for additional communities to enable their development and potential future entry to the Fairtrade movement. It also created the shift in corporate mindset that enabled Fairtrade to be embraced, bringing a development agenda and the NGO sector into the heart of a multinational company.

REACHING A NEW FAIRTRADE CONSUMER

The Cadbury brand occupies a particularly envious place in the hearts and minds of consumers. It regularly scores highly in the Reader's Digest annual survey of brands that people trust, and research has ranked it as the second most powerful brand in the country beating a number of global brands and national institutions.[18] Its long heritage of values-led behaviour, and of doing responsible things but not shouting from the rooftops about them, is a major contributor to this.

This heritage could quite easily have led to Cadbury making its Fairtrade and Cocoa Partnership moves quietly, behind the scenes. But increasingly the context has changed. Consumers now demand to know what's behind a product.

However, Cadbury is a mainstream brand, as beloved by 'white van man' and 'hoodies', as by the ethical seekers. Through Fairtrade Cadbury was providing all with an easy, affordable option: their favourite chocolate with the same great taste and great value, but with added ethics. Communicating this would be more of a challenge than it might first seem. The aim was to do this in a way that would be accessible to Joe Public not just the ethical elite, and avoid being too self-congratulatory whilst still celebrating the move. Cadbury could be the catalyst to take Fairtrade to a totally new audience.

It also needed to be true to the brand's personality. This was the brand that brought you the bizarre drumming gorilla and strange eyebrow-dancing kids so communications needed to be surprising and entertaining. Just like the rest of the 'glass and a half full' campaigns it aimed to make you smile – this time Ghanaian style. Filmed in cocoa villages it fused traditional and modern Ghanaian pop culture with a good splash of the trademark quirky Cadbury imagination. Cadbury worked with Tinny, Ghana's hottest 'hiplife' music star, to produce an original record called 'Zingolo' (which means 'Enjoy it') with the proceeds from the record going to cocoa growing communities. They also worked with Paulo Nutini who swapped his usual band for a special Ghanaian band as part of the 2010 Fairtrade Fortnight 'Big Swap' campaign. The campaigns are bigger than any preceding Fairtrade campaign, utilising prime time television and industry-leading digital techniques, and through their fun positioning aimed to turn on those turned off by traditional, 'preachy' ethical marketing.

A SUSTAINABLE FUTURE

When Kraft's acquisition of Cadbury was announced in February 2010, one of the key touchstones for employees and consumers was the future of the Cadbury–Fairtrade partnership, and the Cocoa Partnership. It is a mark of the initiative's success that Kraft was swift to make public commitments to continue this work alongside its existing work with the Rainforest Alliance in support of cocoa and coffee farmers.[19] And the broader response from Cadbury's competitors has been to increase their activities in moves which can only be good for the sector. (Mars through their Impact programme to support cocoa farming including a commitment to Rainforest Alliance adoption in their supply chain,[20] and Nestlé through a commitment to Fairtrade for Kit Kat.)[21]

A lot has already changed in the two years since Cadbury decided to look at the issues of cocoa sustainability with a positive glass-and-a-half-full mindset. Many of the challenges have been overcome – from scale to price, to quality, to marketing. And through the Cadbury case, Fairtrade has succeeded in fundamentally changing the landscape and strengthened its hand with multinational companies. Consumer attitudes are also moving faster than ever in Fairtrade's direction. But the true transformation continues on the ground in farming communities, as the Fairtrade promise is built on the foundations of responsible behaviour.

NOTES

1. H.T. Stitzer, 'Tipping the Balance through Principled Capitalism', Presentation to Fairtrade Commercial Conference, 24 September 2009.
2. M. De Lattre-Gasquet, D. Despreaux and M. Barel, 'Prospective de la filière du cacao' (Prospective study of the cocoa commodity channel), *Plantations, Recherche, Développement* 5(6): 423–34, November–December 1998.
3. Stitzer, 'Tipping the Balance'.
4. http://cadburyar2008.production.investis.com/~/media/Files/C/cadbury-ar-2008/pdf/cadbury_ra_13mb_compressed.ashx
5. www.dearcadbury.com/i-know-my-stuff/index.aspx
6. 'Absolute' vs. 'relative' carbon emissions: many companies have commitments to reduce 'relative' carbon emissions, i.e. emissions per tonne of finished product. This means that as production processes become more efficient energy intensity is reduced and less carbon is emitted per tonne. However if a business grows the total amount of carbon emitted may also grow. An 'absolute'

cut commits a business to reduce not only emissions per tonne but also the overall footprint despite any growth. This makes absolute targets more challenging, particularly for a sector such as manufacturing compared to service and retail industries.

7. Stitzer, 'Tipping the Balance'.
8. Fairtrade values.
9. www.dearcadbury.com/i-know-my-stuff/index.aspx
10. www.treecrops.org/
11. http://edition.cnn.com/2008/WORLD/asiapcf/07/06/eco.chocolate/index.html
12. www.cadbury.com/SiteCollectionDocuments/Mapping%20Sustainable%20Production%20in%20Ghanaian%20Cocoa%20Study.pdf
13. www.cocoainitiative.org/
14. www.cadbury.com/SiteCollectionDocuments/Mapping%20Sustainable%20Production%20in%20Ghanaian%20Cocoa%20Study.pdf
15. R.O. Odutwum, *The Growth and Poverty Reduction Strategy – GPRS II (2008–2009)*, National Development Planning Commission, www.ndpc.gov.gh/GPRS/The%20Architects%20by%20DR%20ADUTWUM.pdf
16. www.cadbury.com/ourresponsibilities/cadburycocoapartnership/Pages/cadburycocoapartnership.aspx
17. Fairtrade Labelling Organizations International, 'Generic Fairtrade Trade Standards', www.fairtrade.net/fileadmin/user_upload/content/GTS_Aug09_EN.pdf
18. Hall & Partners, 2010.
19. www.kraftfoods.co.uk/kraft/page?siteid=kraft-prd&locale=uken1&PagecRef=2526&Mid=41
20. www.mars.com/global/principle-in-action/impact.aspx
21. www.thecocoaplan.com/

8
Honesty, Openness and Social Responsibility

John Bowes

The Co-operative Group effectively pioneered the development of fair trade in the UK. Whilst the early marketing of fair trade products was essentially focused on alternative trading organisations, such as Oxfam, it was the Co-op who recognised the potential in the mainstream market. They seized the initiative and, between 1996 and 2003, they stole a march on all of their competitors by investing in an ambitious programme which, subsequently, became a catalyst for the growth of the whole sector.

The Co-op supported the concept of fair trade from the very start of this period. It began stocking Cafédirect, one of the first products to carry the FAIRTRADE Mark, as early as 1992. In 1996 it linked up with the Fairtrade Foundation to develop a monitoring scheme aimed at delivering fair working conditions for workers in factories producing Co-op brand products around the world. The following year it became a founder member of the Ethical Trading Initiative, an organisation committed to improving the quality of life for workers in the developing world. In 1998 Co-op 99 Tea became the first mainstream food product to be marketed using ethical trade criteria.[1] And, by this time, all Co-op stores, even the very smallest, were stocking Fairtrade products.

But the Co-op really left its mark on the fair trade movement with a series of seminal initiatives at the start of the new century. Dramatic and high profile developments which, taken together, carried fair trade into the UK mainstream and kick-started the so-called fair trade revolution.

In the millennium year the Co-op became the first UK retailer to introduce Fairtrade bananas. They were sourced from Volta River Estates in Ghana, with the assistance of AgroFair, and marketed under the OKE brand. This was a dramatic new development. Bananas were not only the top selling fruit in the UK they were also the number one KVI or known value item, reflecting their huge volume sales and high frequency of purchase. The introduction of the FAIRTRADE Mark to bananas removed, at a stroke, any doubts about the potential for fair trade to move into the mainstream market.

In the same year the Co-op engineered a paradigm shift in the whole market by the introducing of the UK's first own brand Fairtrade product. This one product, a simple milk chocolate bar, sourced with the aid of the Day (Divine) Chocolate Company, may, in retrospect, be seen as the single most important market development for fair trade products in the UK. It established the format and set the pattern for a decade of rapid and sustained growth. Over the course of the next few years the UK retail trade embraced fair trade through the development of own brand ranges.

Two years later the Co-op's relationship with Divine, and Kuapa Kokoo in Ghana, resulted in another positive twist in the fair trade development story. They announced that they had 'chosen chocolate as the focus for making Fairtrade mainstream because of the stark – even obscene –

contrast between the pleasure derived form eating it and the suffering that goes into making it'.[2] Recognising the misery, exploitation, and impoverishment of West African cocoa growers their response was to convert the whole of their own brand block chocolate range to Fairtrade. The Co-op would simply no longer put its name to a chocolate product unless it could be certain that its growers had been fairly treated.

In 2003 the Co-op went a stage further when it adopted exactly the same policy for its own brand coffee range. It responded to an Oxfam report entitled *Mugged: Poverty in Your Coffee Cup*, which highlighted the dreadful plight of an estimated 25 million people dependent on coffee in the world's poorest countries, by switching its entire own brand coffee range to Fairtrade.[3] This was a high volume product operating in a highly competitive retail environment. This one move, at a stroke, increased the value of Fairtrade coffee sold in the UK by 15 per cent.[4] The Co-op was taking a serious commercial risk. It was undertaking to pay more for its coffee, a significant part of its retail business, in the belief and expectation that its customers would respond positively to its ethical stance.

The Co-op was the first UK supermarket to convert entire own brand categories to Fairtrade. And the importance of this concept and development can hardly be understated. Firstly, because it demonstrated that fair trade need no longer be contained to the niche product slot within the range: it was no longer just a token gesture to an ethical minority; it was becoming the standard by which others would be judged. Secondly, because it became a model which other retailers would copy; over the past few years Sainsbury's, Marks & Spencer and Waitrose have all carried out category conversions in key commodity areas. And, thirdly, from a producer's perspective, it offered the prospect of more stable and sustained trading relationship with a partner actively committed to developing fair trade sales:

> When a supermarket switches an entire product category to Fairtrade it makes a greater investment in ensuring there will be a reliable source of supply year round. Most supermarkets have tried to work with their existing supply base to get producers registered with the Fairtrade Labelling Organisation, but sometimes suppliers are unable or unwilling to do so. In such cases the supermarkets have to invest in locating new sources and building up supply relationships. Importantly, they have also adjusted their pricing strategies to ensure that the product categories do not become uncompetitive, including reducing profit margins where they think consumers will not be willing to absorb additional costs. Although it is hoped that the investment and loss of margin will be recouped in extra sales (as well as in publicity and brand value through association with Fairtrade), by default this also implies that more effort will be made to promote Fairtrade and ensure the product sells. This tends to create a virtuous circle of investment and commitment, as association of the supermarket brand with Fairtrade becomes stronger and it becomes more difficult for the supermarket to contemplate walking away.[5]

In this context, it is perhaps not surprising that the Co-op also led the way in promoting the whole concept of fair trade. In the autumn of 2003, the Co-op produced a bespoke fair trade television commercial as part of its award winning 'Creatures' campaign. The advertisement, which was focused on its own brand chocolate, reinforcing its commitment to the trading relationship with Kuapa Kokoo, received heavyweight national exposure. Positive reactions, in terms of both sales and customer feedback, encouraged the Co-op to go one stage further by adapting the commercial to support its main Christmas campaign. As a result, the fair trade message was transmitted simultaneously to millions of people, on prime time television, during the most critical trading period of the year. This was the first time that fair trade had received such high profile exposure. In retrospect it is difficult to underestimate the impact that this initiative had on raising awareness amongst both customers and with other retailers. Once again the Co-op had delivered a seismic shift in market potential. Fair trade had quite definitely arrived in the mainstream.

Taken together this series of groundbreaking initiatives represented an astonishing achievement. Such was the speed and magnitude of the changes being delivered by the Co-op that it is tempting to conclude that this one organisation, almost single-handedly, launched fair trade into the grocery market and, in so doing, became the platform upon which the fair trade revolution has subsequently been built. But what was the motivation? Back in the mid 1990s the Co-op was a business with some serious problems, so why did it choose to go out on a limb for fair trade?

The Co-op's origins date back to the middle of the nineteenth century in the industrial north-west. There had been many early attempts to establish businesses and communities based on cooperative principles but, by common consent, the founding of the Rochdale Equitable Pioneers Society, on 15 August 1844, represents the birth of the modern cooperative movement. Times were desperate; working conditions were poor, wages were low and declining, unemployment was high and average life expectancy was just 21 years. What followed was perhaps the greatest example of working class self-help in the history of the western world. Influenced by the ideas of Robert Owen and the Chartist movement, and moved by idealism as much as hunger, 28 men set up their first store in

Toad Lane, Rochdale, Lancashire.[6] The venture was a success and became the template for other cooperative enterprises. By 1881 there were 971 societies with more than half a million members, and by the turn of the century combined membership was 1.7 million in 1,439 societies nationwide.

What made the Rochdale model so influential was not just its trading success but also the principles upon which the business was founded. These included open membership, democratic control, distribution of surplus in proportion to trade (the cooperative dividend), promotion of education, and political and religious neutrality.[7] They were the basis upon which the cooperative movement was built and have proved to be essentially resilient over time. Even today the Co-operative Group acknowledges that its business practice is guided by the values and principles of the movement:

> Co-operatives are based on the values of self-help, self-responsibility, democracy, equality, equity and solidarity. In the tradition of their founders, co-operative members believe in the ethical values of honesty, openness, social responsibility, and caring for others.[8]

From a simple commercial perspective these values and principles represent the essential difference between the Co-op and all of its major competitors. While the major retail multiple chains must strive to meet the requirements of their shareholders and the financial community in the City, the Co-op is responsible to a membership committed to a defined set of ethical values. It follows that whilst some of the multiples may embrace aspects of the ethical agenda, they presumably do so because they recognise its commercial potential in an era when concerns about these issues are front of mind. The Co-op, in contrast, embraces these issues because they are part of its DNA; they are its raison d'être.

This differential advantage served the cooperative movement well during its early days. It became a huge business with interests in many different fields. Even as late as the mid 1970s it held more than a 20 per cent share of the UK grocery market. But the abolition of retail price maintenance in 1963, which allowed retailers to compete openly on price for the very first time, had exposed the people's business to serious multiple competition. The advantage of the customer dividend was eroded by the emergence of fierce price competition and new promotional techniques such as Green Shield trading stamps. As a result many cooperative societies abandoned the traditional dividend as they struggled to survive. The Co-operative Wholesale Society (now the Co-operative Group) in Manchester, acting as the central federal organisation, attempted to stem the tide by persuading the retail cooperative societies, faced with the scale and efficiency of the retail multiple chains, to pool their buying potential and invest in nationally organised promotional and television campaigns. These sought to reflect cooperative values with sign-off lines such as 'Caring and Sharing' and 'People Who Care'. But, in reality, any commitment to the ethical agenda ran pretty thin during this period, as the business struggled in the face of unprecedented competition.

The emerging breed of multiple retailers were highly focused, centrally controlled and efficient organisations. In contrast, the cooperative movement was trapped by its own history; it was not one organisation but many. And the real authority was invested in the autonomous retail societies and not in the central federal organisation. As a result its buying and marketing power was dissipated and its focus tended to be introspective as management in both Manchester and in the retail societies struggled to arrive at any consistent strategic consensus. Market share plummeted.

Clearly, this could not continue. During the late 1980s and early 1990s the Co-operative Wholesale Society switched its main focus from manufacturing to retailing and began a process of merging with ailing retail societies. And, in 1993, in a revolutionary move, it established the Co-operative Retail Trading Group; bringing together the marketing and buying for its own retail operations with those of three other major societies. This was the start of the process which would, within a decade, bring together the Co-op's food buying interests and invest authority in a single trading team. This process was to have immediate and far reaching consequences for the Co-op's support for the emerging ethical agenda.

With the central federal cooperative now effectively in control of the marketing agenda it was finally possible to act. In January 1993, coincident with the creation of the Co-operative Trading Group, the Consumer Issues Group was set up. This internal committee included senior management representatives, from different disciplines across the business, who all shared a commitment to cooperative values and principles. The intention was to establish the Co-op as the UK's most ethical retailer and in 1995 the business went public with the concept of responsible retailing. Based on a major survey of its members the Co-op concluded that their customers 'didn't just want food to look and taste nice':

> They saw that if the way food was made meant it was cruel to farm animals, bad for the environment, contained questionable chemicals and exploited poor people in poor countries, then it was ultimately bad for them. People were becoming hungry for food that was sourced, produced, and sold with integrity.[9]

What followed was a series of initiatives stretching across the whole ethical agenda.

In 1994 it became the first retailer to support the RSPCA Freedom Food scheme to improve animal welfare standards for animals at all stages of the food chain; working with the charity to develop the concept and supporting its launch with a range of Co-op brand Freedom Food products. A year later it became the first retailer to label eggs 'intensively produced'; reflecting customers' concern about honest labelling. It introduced its Community Dividend scheme to fund projects to the benefit of local communities; banned genetically modified ingredients from Co-op brand food products; launched Britain's first 100% degradable plastic carrier bag, to help reduce landfill waste; and, of course, it wholeheartedly embraced the fair trade agenda.

In 1997 the Co-operative Group staved off a predatory takeover attempt. The failed bid had been actively supported by two senior managers in the Co-op's food business. This event had a fortuitous outcome. It brought forward the implementation of a strategic review which now saw the group focus on its core strength in convenience store retailing; and responsible retailing was given a central role within the marketing strategy for the business. In addition, the departure of two top managers resulted in key positions within the revised structure being filled by members of the Consumer Issues Group. By the close of that year the respective heads of food retail, marketing, Co-op brand, public relations and corporate affairs were all original members of the group and active supporters of the responsible retailing agenda.

These people, both collectively and as individuals, now had a serious level of authority within the business and were able to drive the ethical agenda forward. But although they had an empathy with responsible retailing they were employed as professional managers. They recognised the commercial opportunity in positioning the Co-op as the UK's most ethical business. The developments they engendered were not acts of faith but initiatives based on commercial calculation. Their objective was to promote the Co-op as a brand by developing a twenty-first century expression of its unique origins and its cooperative values and principles.

There is no fault in this. Indeed, it demonstrates a high degree of commercial perspicacity. But within any organisation managers come and go. Careers rise and fall. Managers are not permanent fixtures. And when there are management changes there is always the possibility of a change in policy. This is a given; it is practically inevitable. Therefore, in most large businesses a commitment to an ethical policy might be expected to have longevity no greater than the presiding chief executive's span of employment at the head of the organisation. But, in this respect, the Co-op is different too.

The Co-operative Group is a membership-based organisation with over a million members, many of whom are active in its affairs. Membership is open to anyone with just a pound to invest, as long as they are committed to cooperative values and principles, and members can put themselves forward for election to the various tiers of the Group's representative democracy, including the Co-operative Group board. They have the key governance role. While the management are left to get on with running a highly professional business the membership, through the board, has ultimate control on the appointment of the top management team and the direction of the organisation.

The Co-op's membership has always been strongly supportive of the ethical agenda. In 1994 the Co-operative

Group conducted the biggest ever study of consumer attitudes into the ethics of the food industry when it surveyed 30,000 of its members. They were very concerned about a whole range of issues including support for the developing world, honest labelling, farm animal welfare, wildlife, pollution and packaging. Ten years later, in 2004, it repeated the exercise and found that attitudes had substantially hardened. Co-op members wanted and expected higher standards of integrity from the food industry. But the most startling feature of the results was not simply the increasing level of concern about ethical issues but the absolute magnitude of that concern. Support for initiatives to assist growers in the developing world had increased by 45 per cent, and embraced a stunning 80 per cent of those surveyed in 2004.[10]

This survey was the basis of a second stage in the development of the Co-op's responsible retailing agenda. It went forward with a series of measurable commitments across six areas of concern identified by the survey: honest labelling, food integrity, animal welfare and testing, environment and sustainability, support for local communities, and globalisation and poverty reduction. In this latter context the Co-op set itself the target of doubling its own brand range of Fairtrade products and finding new ways of using Fairtrade ingredients in standard supermarket lines.

Most Fairtrade products are commodities, such as coffee, tea and bananas, and are by definition entirely Fairtrade. However, the Fairtrade Foundation recognised that there was an opportunity for other products, where the ingredients might be a mixture of Fairtrade (such as sugar, honey or vanilla) and ingredients sourced more locally (such as flour, milk or eggs). By allowing the certification of these so-called composite products, where at least 50 per cent of the total ingredients are sourced from Fairtrade certified sources, the Foundation opened up significant new opportunities for producers in the developing world. Given the Co-op's continued commitment to the fair trade agenda it is not surprising that it became an early innovator with composite products. New product introductions have included Christmas puddings, mince pies, Easter eggs, ice lollies, chocolate cakes, choc chip shortbread, cereal bars, honey ale and hand-finished chocolates

There have also been further developments with major commodity lines. In 2007 the Co-op introduced the world's first Fairtrade grapefruit and it was also the first supermarket to introduce Fairtrade cotton carrier bags. The following year it became the first UK retailer to convert its entire own-brand hot beverage range to Fairtrade, adding Co-op tea and hot chocolate to existing Fairtrade ranges on coffee. It now sells 230 Fairtrade products in its food stores, of which 146 are own brand.[11]

In the meantime the Co-op's high street competition has not stood still. While support from the Co-op was the bedrock upon which fair trade's initial success was based, entering fully into the mainstream demanded the participation of the major multiples. All four of the major multiples had an early flirtation with the concept but the breakthrough came in 2004 when Tesco introduced a comprehensive range of own brand Fairtrade products. By the end of 2005, Tesco was stocking 90 Fairtrade lines and was able to claim that its customers bought one in three of Fairtrade products sold through supermarkets in the UK. From almost a standing start it had become the market leader for Fairtrade products in less than two years.[12]

This achievement has since been dwarfed by Sainsbury's. In January 2008 they took the decision to convert the whole of their banana range to Fairtrade. Bananas have huge volumes. This represented a serious investment and only Waitrose followed suit. At a single stroke, Sainsbury's became the biggest retailer by value of Fairtrade products in the UK. They now have more than 200 own brand products which carry the FAIRTRADE Mark.

Since the Co-op Group began to focus its food business on convenience stores it has done very well. The business has grown quite dramatically through a process of merger and acquisition, and has reported an almost uninterrupted improvement in its financial performance over the last ten years or so. Following its acquisition of Somerfield it is now the UK's fifth largest food retailer with a market share of about 8 per cent. However, its focus on small stores means that it carries a much smaller range than the other large retailers. In this context, the fact that it stocks almost as many Fairtrade products as Sainsbury's, and more than every other retailer, is a testimony to its on-going commitment to fair trade.

The Co-operative Group's latest sustainability report estimates that

more than 7.5 million people – farmers, workers and their families – across approximately 60 developing countries, benefit from the international Fairtrade system, of which it is estimated that over 150,000 people benefited from The Co-operative Food's sales of Fairtrade products in 2008.[13]

This is a laudable achievement. It is also, in probability, a considerable underestimate of the Co-op's contribution to fair trade.

The Co-op's commitment to the ethical agenda has been driven by its values and principles, its unique history, some inspired management, and an active membership base. Its achievement can't be measured simply in terms of number of products and value of sales. It took the initiative and demonstrated what could be achieved. It provided the inspiration for the whole market; creating a virtuous circle of momentum and commitment; a focal point for activists; and a benchmark for the rest of the retail industry. It is probably an overstatement to say that without the Co-op fair trade would have remained the preserve of alternative trading organisations. But what is absolutely certain is that without the Co-op the fair trade revolution would have taken a great deal longer to get started. Today, the Co-op is generally recognised as being the UK's most ethical brand. Its pioneering role in developing fair trade underpins and gives credence to that accolade.

NOTES

1. *Shopping With Attitude*, Co-operative Group, 2004, p. 18.
2. *Chocolate*, Co-operative Group, 2002, p. 2.
3. *Mugged: Poverty in Your Coffee Cup*, Oxfam, 2002. See www.oxfam.org.uk/resources/papers/mugged.html
4. *Coffee*, Co-operative Group, 2003, p. 4.
5. Sally Smith, *For Love or Money? Fairtrade Business Models in the UK Supermarket Sector*, 3rd Fair Trade International Symposium, 14–16 May 2008, Montpellier, France.
6. Johnston Birchall, *Co-op: The People's Business*, Manchester University Press, 1994, pp. 34–8.
7. Ibid., pp. 54–5.
8. *Sustainability Report 2008/9*, Co-operative Group, 2009.

9. *Shopping With Attitude*, Co-operative Group, 2004, p. 5.
10. Ibid., p. 7.
11. *Sustainability Report 2008/9*, Co-operative Group, 2009, p. 15.
12. John Bowes and David Croft, 'Organic and Fair Trade Crossover and Convergence', in Simon Wright and Diane McCrea (eds), *The Handbook of Organic and Fair Trade Food Marketing*, Blackwell, 2007, p. 270.
13. *Sustainability Report 2008/9*, Co-operative Group, 2009, p. 15.

9
Banana Breakthrough

Matt North

My first involvement and real understanding of the FAIRTRADE Mark began in 2005 when I became the banana and citrus fruit buyer at Sainsbury's, 17 years after originally joining the supermarket chain as a trainee manager. During this time I had worked in the Retail, Property, Marketing and subsequently in its Trading divisions, meeting and working with customers and suppliers alike. This was all pretty straightforward commercial stuff until I was fortunate enough to meet banana growers in the developing world.

By 2006, one in five Sainsbury's customers was already purchasing Fairtrade bananas, choosing to purchase the Fairtrade pack which was sold in nearly all of its stores. Our Fairtrade bananas at this time were all sourced from the islands of St Lucia, St Vincent and the Dominican Republic; in total about a third of the bananas we imported from these countries were being sold as Fairtrade in our stores. The rest of our 'conventional' bananas were sourced from Costa Rica and Belize. Sales and customer awareness were definitely growing but we were still not able to sell all of the Fairtrade bananas available from the growers. Notwithstanding this,

I felt generally pleased that our Fairtrade banana sales were higher than the other UK multiples such as Tesco and Asda.

As a produce buyer at Sainsbury's there is a necessity to visit some of your major suppliers around the world to gain an understanding and appreciation of the products you are purchasing. This is firstly informative, but it also enables you to make tough commercial decisions based on the quality and efficiencies you view at source. In May 2006, I was fortunate enough to go on a sourcing trip to Belize, Costa Rica, Dominican Republic and the islands of St Lucia and St Vincent – in fact my entire banana supply base, in the space of just ten days.

The Sainsbury's banana supply base constituted Fyffes in Costa Rica and Belize, Mack Multiples in Costa Rica and the Dominican Republic, and Windward Bananas supplying from the islands of St Lucia and St Vincent.[1] This supply base, I felt, gave an excellent geographical spread with large 'Dollar Fruit' being imported from Latin America and Belize and with Fairtrade and organic fruit coming from the islands.[2]

The first stop in my banana education was the former British colony in Belize, the predominant source for Fyffes in serving the Sainsbury's business. The banana industry in Belize was a major employer for the people of the country with the production being largely controlled by The Belize Banana Company. Bananas in Belize are usually grown on large plantations and are typically owned by American farmers who spend most of the year in the country managing the production. Fyffes, for their part, employ a country manager who will ensure growers are operating to the standards expected of UK supermarkets.

During the three days we spent touring farms in Belize it was very clear that the standard of living was far lower than anyone experiences in developed countries. Education, healthcare and a good standard of housing were not things the population could come to expect as a given right. As we came across row upon row of shacks, and very basic accommodation, I began to ask questions about the living standards that workers could expect, and what could be done to improve the situation.

As a relatively 'hard-nosed', commercially focused supermarket buyer I was used to asking questions about productivity, freight rates and yield. Now I began to ask very different questions. How many children go to school? What childcare facilities are there? How much does a bus cost? How much does it cost to build a house?

To the credit of Fyffes and the plantation owners they happily accommodated my enquiries and gave me an insight into the problems the industry faced. I was even shown recent developments where Fyffes had invested their own money to improve the infrastructure for local communities. But the sheer scale of the challenges required radically different solutions. When I returned to the comparative luxury of my hotel I started to do the sums.

A typical house in Belize would cost as little as $10,000 to build, at the then exchange rates this equated to about £6,000. At this time Sainsbury's were purchasing around 140,000 cases or some 2.5 million kilogrammes of bananas a week. Even an additional 'grower' premium of 1p a kilo would enable £25,000 to be returned every week, enough for four houses. I was now starting to think there maybe something in this idea.

As the trip moved to Costa Rica, I continued to have the same thoughts. Costa Rica was far more developed than Belize but similar challenges faced the banana workers and their families. Although the Rainforest Alliance mark was starting to develop in Costa Rica, the more I reviewed this I felt clear that it wasn't addressing the key social needs of the communities whose livelihoods depended upon the banana industry.

By the time we had reached the Caribbean islands of the Dominican Republic and St Lucia I was becoming obsessed with one question: could Sainsbury's make a real difference to these communities?

But there was already a difference for some of the communities in these islands. St Lucia, St Vincent and, to a lesser extent, the Dominican Republic had seen many growers gain Fairtrade accreditation. The simple difference for Fairtrade growers was they were given a guaranteed minimum price and an additional $1 a case social premium. As a group of growers they were then able to democratically decide how the premium was spent within their communities. The only provision being that this money was invested in social projects, such as housing, healthcare or education.

So now my questions became more focused on Fairtrade. How does the money get spent? How do you decide which project takes priority? What would you do if you had more money to spend? How much of your crop is sold as Fairtrade?

In my own mind I had already bought into the fact that the Fairtrade model seemed to work and it was making a difference to communities in these islands. The next question to resolve was how could we substantially increase Fairtrade sales and ensure that even more people enjoyed the benefits.

Once back at Sainsbury's offices in Holborn, central London, I continued to do my sums. I wanted to understand the scale of the challenge and the size of the prize; basically what difference could we make?

The UK Fairtrade banana market was worth in the region of £30 million, of which we enjoyed a share of nearly 40 per cent. But less than a fifth of the bananas we sold were Fairtrade at that time. The farmers in St Lucia were currently unable to sell even half of their crop as Fairtrade as there wasn't sufficient global demand for it. I looked at the current range of products we sold: five different packs and a loose banana offer, and over 60 per cent of the volume was sold as loose. It became obvious that to make a huge difference we would have to convert all our products to Fairtrade. But how could that be done? Even if we could persuade our customers to support this, could we even find enough Fairtrade bananas to sell to meet the demand?

To further develop this idea I needed to now understand how easy it was for a grower to become Fairtrade accredited and how difficult it would be to really increase the volume of Fairtrade bananas we sourced.

The only way to do this was through really engaging with the Fairtrade Foundation in the UK. Mark Varney had responsibility at the Foundation for developing Fairtrade fruit and it was clear from the outset he also had ambitious plans for developing Fairtrade sales on bananas. Mark was rightly proud of what had been achieved but now all the retailers had a Fairtrade pack on the shelves, where was it going to go next? I soon started to learn about some of the challenges we faced in changing our supply.

The situation I had seen in the Caribbean was relatively unique as Fairtrade had been able to gain prominence due to all the small farmers on the islands. The typical farmer may only farm around one hectare compared to the thousand-hectare plantations in Costa Rica. Fairtrade classified growers as either small producers, who controlled their own production, or plantations with hired labour. So it had been relatively easy for these farmers to gain small producer status within Fairtrade Labelling Organizations International (FLO).

The process for large producers was much more complicated and time consuming. They had to clearly show, amongst other things, that the workers were actively involved in democratically determining how and where the Fairtrade premiums were spent. To ensure this was managed effectively workers needed to have properly elected joint bodies to ensure that everyone's views were considered. In most cases the body would be formed from trade union representatives. It was also clear that the inspection and accreditation process was rather time consuming and could often run into many months. At this time over two thirds of the volume Sainsbury's sold came from these large plantations.

Although Mark continued to remain positive I was becoming concerned whether a full conversion would ever be a possibility for a business the scale of Sainsbury's. At this point I started to think of other potential socially responsible trading models.

The Rainforest Alliance mark was much easier to achieve but no real social benefits were returned to the communities. Alternatively, Waitrose had their own Foundation for growers in South Africa but when I investigated this scheme it seemed fairly complicated and, more importantly, it didn't seem to be independently audited in the same way that Fairtrade was. If Sainsbury's introduced its own Foundation would customers believe the benefits were real or see it as a cynical marketing ploy? Furthermore, would it then be competing against the existing FAIRTRADE Mark?

The more I looked into the question it seemed that the only way to guarantee fair returns, and ensure the social premium was returned to the communities in a way which matched their own priorities, was through the FAIRTRADE Mark. So the only way to achieve a real difference was through Fairtrade; and the only way to achieve this with real scale was by converting our entire range of bananas to Fairtrade. To achieve this we would need to massively change our existing supply base and I would need to obtain agreement from my bosses at Sainsbury's that it would be a sensible thing to do. It seemed I was becoming a 'Fairtrade evangelist'.

Initially I went to the then fruit category manager at Sainsbury's and explained what I had seen on my visit and my potential thoughts on how Sainsbury's could make a difference through Fairtrade. Although he could see the merits in my suggestion it was clear that there were a number of serious commercial issues to address.

Bananas were the number one sales line in volume at Sainsbury's, at the front of every shop, and as a consequence, in nearly every shopper's basket. Back then, customers had a perception that Sainsbury's was more expensive than Tesco, Asda and Morrisons, so it was a business necessity to ensure all of the most popular products were at price parity with our competitors. If we passed on the additional cost of Fairtrade to our customers we would need to charge an extra 5p a kilo. This would be impossible commercially. If we made the investment ourselves we would be faced with a bill of around £4 million a year. Clearly, there were difficulties.

But I wasn't going to give up the idea easily and so I continued to challenge people within the business. Karen Schenstrom, the Business unit director for Fresh Foods, could definitely see the benefits and appreciated my passion for the idea. I even went to Mike Coupe, the Trading director. Everyone could see the merits and wanted to help but there was real concern about the cost and the timing. It's important to remember that, at this time, the investment in moving bananas to Fairtrade was equivalent to 2 per cent of the company's operating profit.

SO WHAT CHANGED?

I had been approached by Tesco to take on a buying role with them. To me it was a fantastic offer and closer to my home, and although I had always loved my time at Sainsbury's it felt just too good to turn down. I suppose armed with the knowledge that I had another job opportunity available it enabled me to go for broke on my Fairtrade plans.

At the Sainsbury's Charity Ball, I pitched my idea directly to Justin King, the chief executive. In reality I had probably drunk a little too much and just thought, 'what the hell, I'm probably leaving anyway!' In some respects, it could have been considered career suicide; it certainly would have been when I joined Sainsbury's in 1988. But this was a different company now and Justin was actively encouraging new ideas to be brought to him; perhaps not always this directly though.

Back in the office I nervously opened an email from Justin. Had I overstepped the mark? Was my departure going to be brought forward? No, he wanted further details of my proposals. I felt so excited. I quickly responded with my thoughts, the benefits, the costs and the challenges we would have to overcome. Within hours I received a simple, concise email: 'take us to a place on our no1 product that others would find hard to match'.

So in July 2006 Project Perry commenced with the target of converting all Sainsbury's bananas to Fairtrade within the next year.[3] As usual with these initiatives, the delivery would require a lot of hard work from the supply base.

The biggest challenge we faced was simply securing the necessary volume in relative secrecy. If news of our intentions got out it was clear that Marks & Spencer, Waitrose and the Co-op might all easily steal our thunder; in comparison with Sainsbury's their volumes were so small it would be easy for them to source the volume they would have required. Although this would make no difference to the benefits we would be able to pass on to the communities, we would have lost the recognition I felt we deserved from all our endeavours. Nobody was going to remember who came second in this race.

Sainsbury's sold approximately 145,000 cases of bananas a week of which, at any one time, a maximum would be 25,000 cases of Fairtrade. The total UK Fairtrade banana market, at this time, only represented 60,000 cases. To secure the additional volume we required it would be necessary to convert 120,000 cases to Fairtrade inside a year.

Looking at our existing supply base we had three main challenges. Firstly, in the Caribbean islands we had to convert nearly every grower to Fairtrade. This seemed an absolutely enormous task but Roy Hugh, the sales and marketing director of Windward Bananas in the UK, did an amazing job in selling the vision to his company, the individual grower organisations and the individual growers. Although the task he faced was enormous I never had a moment of concern that he would not be able to deliver on his promises.

Secondly, it was clear that we would need to switch away from the Fyffes source in Belize, the communities that first gave me the inclination to try to make a difference. However hard we looked at the situation and discussed options within the Fairtrade Foundation and FLO it was clear that the ownership structure in Belize was simply incompatible with Fairtrade.[4] In my experience Fyffes' understanding of the banana market is second to none and David Flynn, Paul Armstrong and the team at Fyffes were quickly able to deliver an alternative.

One of the strengths of Fyffes as an organisation, is that it sources bananas from a number of geographical areas. Fyffes has a long-standing trading relationship with Uniban, a producer cooperative in Colombia. It was recognised that Colombia represented the source that would be most likely to comply with FLO's requirements for bananas. Colombian banana production has both plantation and smallholder production. A number of farms in Colombia had already converted to Fairtrade albeit the volumes available from these farms were relatively small and would not be sufficient to meet Sainsbury's needs. However, a number of producer groups had expressed an interest to convert to Fairtrade. Fyffes provided Uniban with the necessary 'letter of intent' and the conversion programme was instigated. Representatives from Uniban worked tirelessly for a number of months ensuring the farms would meet the necessary requirements.

There were a number of hurdles to overcome, not least the pace at which the FLO certification process occurs. With the support of Fyffes and the Fairtrade Foundation in the UK, a number of the farm audits were fast-tracked.

Having secured the necessary volume to meet Fyffes' contracted volume commitments to Sainsbury's, they then had to reschedule their shipping arrangements to the UK. Historically fruit from Colombia had been marketed in Continental Europe, and fruit from Belize and Costa Rica had been marketed in the UK. Fyffes rescheduled their vessels with the introduction of a direct service from Colombia to Portsmouth on a weekly basis. David Flynn, managing director of Fyffes in the UK, had practically instigated the change of the whole European supply of bananas to accommodate our request.

Finally we had to organise the conversion of Caribana, Mack's banana supplier in Costa Rica, to Fairtrade. This was potentially the biggest problem we were likely to face in the duration of the whole project. For plantations to comply with Fairtrade requirements they really needed their workers to belong to a trade union but, due to historical labour disputes in the banana industry in Costa Rica, unions had been left with limited powers and dwindling membership numbers. To ensure Caribana were to be able to gain Fairtrade status it would be necessary for the owner and the management of Caribana and the unions to come to an agreement over ways of working. We tried long and hard to reach agreement. We held meetings in the UK involving Alistair Smith of Banana Link, the unions, the Fairtrade Foundation and Elliot Mantle, the Banana director of Mack Multiples.[5]

Alistair, Elliot and I even flew out to Costa Rica to help mediate in sessions between the unions and the management team at Caribana and to sell the merits of Fairtrade. Ultimately these efforts were to prove futile and as a consequence our longstanding trading relationship came to an end.

Although unsuccessful I am left with an amazing memory of Alistair Smith and Jack Loeb Jr, the managing director of Caribana, enjoying a beer and pizza together. Over the previous years they would never have spoken and probably only communicated through legal letters. Alistair Smith is an amazing person and he certainly won my admiration for his tireless campaigning for all the disadvantaged people in the banana industry.

That left a massive hole in supply and Mack needed to work fast to secure enough Fairtrade fruit to enable Sainsbury's to meet their launch date. Fortunately Mack was working with an exporter in Ecuador who was already supplying the company with bananas into the wholesale markets. They also had access to a large volume of Fairtrade bananas that filled the majority of the requirement. With this, added to the increasing volumes from Dominican Republic, they had sufficient to cover the company's volume commitment to Sainsbury's. Whilst this had enabled Mack to meet the initial deadline, there was an issue with quality as the majority of this supply was from smaller growers, who were potentially less consistent.

That led Mack to Colombia where discussions with a large scale producer about becoming Fairtrade certified had begun about six months before we made our Fairtrade decision. Banafrut is a private, independent company with 34 farms covering 3,400 hectares, producing 7.5 million cartons per year. Due to its size, Banafrut needed to apply for Fairtrade certification through Plantation status rather than Small Producer certification. That in itself presented different challenges.

Joint bodies needed to be set up on each farm. The local trade union needed to be brought on board. Unlike the Costa Rican experience, the relationship between the workers, the unions and Banafrut were excellent and the local union accepted Fairtrade as a very important step forward in improving worker conditions. The process was time consuming but Banafrut now has ten farms fully certified as Fairtrade.

Operation Perry had commenced in July 2006 and after seven months of pretty tireless work by the Sainsbury's team, which included David Meller for corporate responsibility and Innogen Hall assuring technical standards, by January 2007 we were now in a position to announce our plans to the wider world.

A joint press release was issued between the Fairtrade Foundation and Sainsbury's advising that we planned to convert all the bananas we sold to Fairtrade by that August. The reaction we received was typically one of amazement and shock in equal measures from anyone involved in the banana industry and the Fairtrade movement. It was difficult for many people to understand the real scale of what we were proposing, and those who did doubted whether it could actually be achieved. Others questioned where the money was coming from and what was in it for us, Sainsbury's. This was due to the fact that we would not be passing the cost increase on to the customers.

In fact, Harriet Lamb, executive director of the Fairtrade Foundation, described the move as 'setting the global Standard for Fairtrade sourcing'.

The press contacted other supermarkets to get their comments. Both Waitrose and the Co-op declared that they planned to do the same, whilst frantically making phone calls to find some Fairtrade fruit. Our move was now becoming a catalyst for change.

Around Fairtrade Fortnight, in February 2007, I was fortunate enough to visit the islands of St Lucia and St Vincent again, with Justin and Harriet, to highlight the real differences Fairtrade was making to the communities of these islands. It was fantastic to watch both Harriet and Justin in action. At times I forgot which one was the Fairtrade banana campaigner; Justin was so positive in his belief that what we were doing was right. During the trip he went from meeting prime ministers, discussing crops with farmers, to showing the local school children how to use a new computer; he gave his time enthusiastically to all of them.

We were left with the simple task of actually delivering our promise of converting our entire range before the August deadline. This we achieved six days ahead of target. We had done it – just!

We had delivered on our promise and achieved the biggest Fairtrade conversion in history. Despite all the initial and understandable reservations the initiative has worked well for Sainsbury's on a commercial level. Market share on bananas increased by about 1 per cent and the company is now responsible for selling over half of the Fairtrade bananas sold in the world. And, most importantly from a Fairtrade perspective, the social premium raised from Fairtrade bananas at Sainsbury's since August 2007 is over £10 million. Returning to my original arithmetic, this is enough money to build nearly 1,700 houses in the developing world. With a lot of help from our suppliers and customers we had been able to make a real difference.

And the success with bananas was only the beginning. The company has since developed this further with other products such as tea, sugar, and cotton. Sainsbury's is now universally recognised as the leading retailer of Fairtrade products in the world.

NOTES

1. Fyffes and Mack are major importers and ripeners of bananas. They import and supply on behalf of Sainsbury's and other major UK retailers.
2. The term 'Dollar fruit', or 'Dollar bananas', refers to fruit from countries in Central and South America which have traditionally

fallen within the influence of the US dollar and whose banana industries have been largely associated with US-based multinational companies.

3. The project was named after Robert Edwin Peary. In 1909 he became the first person to reach the North Pole (or so he claimed), an amazing achievement at that time. So, the project should really have been called 'Peary' but, in practice, the name 'Perry' stuck.

4. The plantations in Belize were typically owned by Americans and had little worker engagement; certainly, there were no worker groups or unions.

5. Banana Link is a small not-for-profit cooperative that campaigns for a fair and sustainable banana trade.

Part III
Future Challenges

10
The Greatest Challenge

Jonathan Rosenthal

ROOTS OF US FAIR TRADE

In the United States, a common misconception prevails that fair trade was invented at the turn of the millennium with the introduction of fair trade certification. Surprisingly, US social justice and trade activists have been looking at changing the rules of trade and debating different theories of how to do that for several centuries. The strategic positioning of abolitionist groups in the 1800s parallels the strategy debates among sectors of the fair trade movement today.

To better understand where the US fair trade movement is, it is useful to look back at where we have been. The debate in the 1800s and now is split into the transformer view, now associated with alternative traders, and the reformer view, which is associated with fair trade labelling. Both sides appear to be increasingly fixed on their differences in the marketplace. The voice of the producers – farmers and craftspeople – is heard less and less as the marketplace conflicts over different strategies, campaigns and small versus large business continue to grow.

The transformers have argued for a radical approach to change in all parts of the food system, in an attempt to create non-corporate partnerships all along the chain from farmer to eater. They believe that business should be focused on building healthy communities, not on accumulating wealth. They further reason that if companies are able to sell a small part of their overall product line as fair trade, then that imparts a fair trade image to their conventional products.

The reformers have used a more incremental approach. They seek to work within existing corporate structures and help companies source products more ethically, hoping to eventually change the way all products are produced. They argue that it is most practical to get companies into the fair trade system and then work with them to convert ever-greater percentages of their product line. Their focus is on building volume as fast as possible for the maximum number of producers.

The transformer approach can be traced back at least as far as efforts of black abolitionists and Quaker groups to end slavery. Small groups of idealists, inspired by English Quaker activists, launched 'Free Produce Initiatives' as early as 1790 to sell slave-free cotton, fruit and vegetables. They sought to topple slavery by using marketplace power. One of the campaigns strove to 'link the sins of the consumer to the sins of the slaveholder'.[1] If people understood that those who bought slave-made goods directly supported involuntary servitude, then providing a more ethical alternative could quickly defeat slavery.

The Free Produce Initiatives grew out of the slavery abolition movement and were championed by early feminists such as Lucretia Mott. However, mainstream abolitionist leaders such as William Lloyd Garrison criticised the initiatives as a distraction, too radical and too focused on individual acts rather than policy changes and large-scale programmes. The slave labour boycotts had limited effect on trade as the boycotts didn't attain significant economies of scale or reach mainstream markets. The last of the Free Produce Initiatives was ended by the Civil War.

BIRTH OF ALTERNATIVE TRADE CRAFTS

A new wave of ethical products appeared 80 years later, just after World War II, imported by what became known as alternative trade organisations (ATOs). This time, faith-based activists from other historic peace churches, the Mennonites and the Church of the Brethren, were the protagonists. Both churches began importing artisan crafts in the late 1940s through ATOs that are now known as Ten Thousand Villages and SERRV. The idea of importing and selling crafts in solidarity with refugees, poor people and struggling communities grew out of a religious commitment to using trade to alleviate poverty. At the outset, the alternative trade movement sought to provide a new form of commerce. These ATOs sold through churches, holiday bazaars and special not-for-profit stores called Third World Shops.

The faith initiatives grew and were replicated during the next few decades in Europe, Australia, the US, Japan and the United Kingdom. During the 1980s, the not-for-profit organisations were joined by a new generation of enterprises in the US, notably Friends of the Third World, Pueblo to People and Equal Exchange. The new groups formed largely out of political solidarity with social movements and grassroots cooperatives. While mostly nonprofit, some operated more in the commercial marketplace than their predecessors.

BIRTH OF ALTERNATIVE TRADE FOOD

In the early 1980s, Friends of the Third World started a food division, Coop Trading, and became the first US importer of ethical coffee. Pueblo to People focused on mail order, but the company could not figure out how to survive as both a nonprofit and as an undercapitalised direct mail company and went out of business. Equal Exchange, a worker cooperative founded in 1986, was the first US for-profit alternative trade company. (The author of this piece was a co-founder.) Its for-profit status, focus on foodstuffs, and overtly political approach distinguished it from traditional alternative traders and businesses. It took several years for the company to build bridges between the different alternative trade groups as the groups strove to create an informal network.

At the same time as this informal network was evolving, what had been an annual gathering hosted by Friends of the Third World evolved into the Fair Trade Federation, a North American trade association. The federation traditionally focused on small handcraft retailers and importers. The federation eventually spun off its educational wing into a separate nonprofit, the Fair Trade Resource Network. At the same time, the International Federation of Alternative Trade – now the World Fair Trade Organization – emerged on the international stage.

The faith-based pioneers continued to concentrate mainly on artisan craft items while steadily professionalising their operations. During the 1980s, coffee became a popular vehicle for alternative traders as well as some more conventional companies with a strong commitment to social change. Many alternative trade groups were inspired by the Nicaraguan Revolution and other liberation movements.

LABELLING EMERGES IN EUROPE

In an attempt to gain market access for coffee farmers and go beyond the niche outlets of the alternative traders, Dutch activists tested several schemes. In 1988, they launched a certification process named 'Max Havelaar', after a popular book in the Netherlands about the abuses of the Dutch coffee system in Indonesia. The move split off the alternative distribution part of the fair trade process from the ethical production component and enabled profit-making companies and brands to market ethical products commercially.

This milestone marked the evolution of alternative trade to fair trade. Coffee sales in the Netherlands increased tenfold in less than two years by broadening the politically radical but tiny alternative trade approach into a product certification programme usable by any company, brand or retailer that complied with the sourcing criteria. Alternative trade coffee that had only been found in Third World Shops and churches became fair trade coffee available everywhere.

Some alternative traders embraced the new initiative and others fought it. Still others cooperated with trade activists and launched an international fair trade seal in an attempt to control and shape the direction of ethical commerce.

In the US, some alternative traders were enthusiastic about the new seal, as they thought it held great distribution promise for small-scale farmers. Some were dismayed as they saw a potential downside: that it would dilute alternative trade ideals and undermine the potential for social change in exchange for moving larger volumes. Equal Exchange tried to harness the power of fair trade certification while resisting the dilution of the ideal by launching a fair trade seal in 1992. Many farmer leaders supported labelling efforts as a way to increase sales. But the unfamiliarity of the ideas made it difficult to raise money. After a year of efforts, the labelling initiative was idled.

In 1993, Equal Exchange was approached by the Smithsonian Migratory Bird Center, which had just concluded that the large-scale mechanisation of coffee production was the biggest cause of the loss of migratory bird habitat. The Center wanted to launch a coffee brand to educate the 60 million US bird lovers about an impending crisis. At the same time, Cultural Survival Enterprises, in partnership with Ben & Jerry's Ice Cream, launched Rainforest Crunch, a nut brittle that was an instant success and helped bring mainstream awareness about the rapidly disappearing Amazon rainforest.

The Equal Exchange workers didn't think they had the capital or size to change the mass market's awareness of bird-friendly coffee. Instead, they persuaded the Smithsonian Center to help launch a super seal. This new effort was coordinated by the Sustainable Coffee Coalition, which joined the forces of conservation groups, progressive coffee companies, trade activists, and other fair trade merchants. The alternative traders worried that saving rainforest trees and migratory birds was easier to promote than fair trade's focus on the poor and that these reform-oriented programmes would overshadow fair trade products.

The second seal attempt didn't work. However, the coalition produced some progress. A small group led by Oxfam America and the Institute for Agriculture and Trade Policy formed TransFair USA, affiliated with a German-based fair trade umbrella, TransFair International. Also, the First Sustainable Coffee Congress was born. The developments put sustainable coffee issues on the agenda in the specialty coffee industry.

LABELLING COMES TO THE US

After a slow start, TransFair USA gained momentum in 1998 by hiring staff. The organisation has grown steadily since then, branching out into other products, though coffee is still the core of its success.

Until the rise of the US branch of TransFair, little ethical coffee was available in the US. The companies involved, most notably Thanksgiving Coffee and Equal Exchange, were intent on creating new brands that challenged the specialty coffee businesses' single-minded focus on cup quality. These new brands looked to overhaul the way coffee was traded by working directly with farmers. This approach meshed with the alternative trade theory of change that looked to make over the role of business to put the interest of all people and communities before capital, stock prices and financial return. But no strong consumer movement or extensive non-government network supported these pioneering small businesses, and the alternative trade groups did not have much capital of their own.

CONFLICTING THEORIES OF CHANGE

TransFair, looking to maximise sales growth, quickly developed a reform-oriented theory of change focused on scale. The group set out to influence some of the nation's largest coffee companies and brands so they could then move to other commodities and products. To work with the large corporations TransFair needed to appear credible and speak the language of boardrooms and not that of progressive political change. However, it needed to build momentum, credibility and some scale before the larger corporations would take the group seriously. TransFair learned how to balance using its credentials from Third World solidarity movements while adopting the lexicon of the corporate world. It developed a vision of becoming a complementary brand, similar to the computer chip maker Intel's successful 'Intel Inside' campaign that was both a sub-brand and an umbrella-brand.

This corporate-centred strategy angered many of the alternative traders and some farmers' organisations that wanted a higher barrier to entry for the corporate players. The activists feared that if big corporations were allowed to enter fair trade with weak standards and no volume requirements, they would crush the alternative traders and their vision of political and social change.

The alternative traders called for at least 5 per cent of overall volume as a minimum threshold, more openness around volumes certified by each company and stronger support for small farmers. TransFair was determined to bring the coffee retailing giant Starbucks into fair trade as it reasoned this would give the organisation the credibility needed to bring fair trade into the mainstream. TransFair declined to create policies that would make it harder for Starbucks and other large corporations to enter fair trade. The split between the transformers and the reformers began to crystallise at this time when, in 2000, TransFair signed an agreement with Starbucks. The volume, however, was small – less than 1 per cent of Starbucks coffee purchases.

TransFair pushed its reform agenda further by looking to bring plantation coffee farms into the certification process. The international fair trade system already had plantation tension as the German TransFair had brought tea plantations into fair trade years earlier, a move that angered small-scale coffee farmers and alternative traders. Farmers and traders worried that if plantations were allowed into fair trade they would use their superior resources to degrade standards and change the fundamental ethic of fair trade.

TransFair leaders were convinced that certifying plantations would ease entry for the corporate coffee merchants that bought from many of the estates and so would grow sales more quickly. They thought this would allow them to bring together organised plantation labourers and small farmers, a feat rarely accomplished in any social movement.

The small farmer coffee groups were upset by TransFair's attempt to work with coffee plantations. After some heated public meetings, TransFair backed down.

A few years later, after pressure from labour unions to work with plantations and eager for another success beyond coffee, TransFair returned to the plantation issue. Now the group looked to bananas. European alternative traders had already certified an African banana plantation that was 25 per cent owned by a workers' trust. TransFair leaders thought this precedent would make plantation bananas easier to market than coffee. The one major nonprofit that had invested deeply in promoting fair trade, Oxfam America, was caught off-guard by this direction.

Oxfam realised that linking its brand with TransFair and therefore potentially with certification of multinational banana estates owned by Chiquita, would put it in an awkward position. So this dominant nonprofit fought the addition of multinational-owned estates to the fair trade banana register. Previously fragmented grassroots groups were able to share their concerns and perspectives and present a unified voice. This put tremendous pressure on TransFair and the estate banana deal collapsed. Several years later it was revived with Dole, and multinational-owned estates were added to the fair trade banana register. The alternative traders were joined by banana unions in their disappointment with the TransFair deal with Dole. The movements working to help poor farm workers and small farmers were further fragmented.[2]

Oxfam America, reflecting on a changed world and the difficulties in fair trade, soon reduced support and funding for fair trade involvement. Even without a strong consumer base and few fair trade programmes, TransFair continued to grow and attract capital and licensees.

CURRENT REALITY AND THE ROAD AHEAD

TransFair accepts the conventional business framework and tries to maximise fair trade sales with whoever can sell the product. This approach created new momentum for fair trade in what had been a weak system with few participants, small budgets and fragile consumer demand. However, the group's emphasis on making fair trade work for corporate brands and retailers made collaboration with fair trade players with an anti-corporate agenda difficult. In the twelve years of TransFair certification, sales have multiplied by a factor of more than 100, yet consumer interest and the number of NGOs engaged in fair trade has not kept pace.

This surge of sales and awareness, coupled with grassroots movement weakening, has frustrated activists and pioneering fair trade companies. Ironically, the broad increase in fair trade awareness has helped boost sales for these alternative trade companies.

Alternative traders have a constant struggle with a basic contradiction. They are building 'new' business models outside of standard business practice yet are also competing to succeed inside of the system they criticise. They have not yet discovered how to strongly differentiate their brands from the corporate fair trade brands. The transformers, like the reformers, end up fixating on incremental growth and expanding awareness of fair trade. When they have developed a large enough presence in a niche, bigger brands and retailers enter the space, often with lower costs, stronger distribution networks and markedly bigger promotional budgets.

The financial crisis that began in 2008 and the maturation of the business cycle have already slowed growth for most progressive companies. Market growth is still lagging, with overall fair trade growth coming mostly from new product introductions and a few huge retail brands, mostly Starbucks.[3] Some flagship fair trade brands will likely begin to slow down and possibly even decline. In the conventional business world, this would be a time in which pioneering brands would be bought by larger brands looking to enter a new niche and buy expertise. Given the anti-corporate stance of many of these brands, however, this appears unlikely on a large scale.

THE SCOPE OF FAIR TRADE IN THE US

Fair trade retail sales and public awareness have grown dramatically in the US in the last 15 years. Retail sales of crafts, clothing and food products marketed by a few dozen alternative traders have grown from less than $100 million in 1996 to more than $1.25 billion[4] of retail sales by hundreds of small, medium and multinational brands. Food has become the dominant category and fair trade food products are available in thousands of retail stores, online and through faith-based organisations.

The engine of growth has been coffee, with 495 coffee roasters and brands selling fair trade coffee in the US in 2010. The purveyors range from tiny micro roasters to Dunkin' Donuts. The lines between the transformers and reformers are blurring as both use the same certification and language. While fair trade coffee has continued to reach new sales levels – 3.5 per cent of total coffee imported into the US in 2009,[5] other fair trade certified products have not had nearly the same success. TransFair is piloting fair trade cotton garments and continually adding new products to keep growth and momentum going. Now it is looking for the next big hit to follow coffee while extending the reach of fair trade deeper into super-coffee brands such as Starbucks and mega-retailers Costco and Walmart.

The marketplace is becoming increasingly crowded with new certifications. On the alternative trade side, the trade association of alternative traders now known as the World Fair Trade Organization (WFTO) is preparing to launch its own certification – of whole organisations. This approach requires that all products sold by a company must be fairly traded, not just one product or line of products. Companies certified by the WFTO must be completely committed to fair trade; they can't just add a fair trade offering to take advantage of current market trends. The organisation is trying to reassert the power of the transformative approach, as reformative labelling initiatives have become the dominant players in the marketplace because of the tremendous growth of labelling.

Even WFTO-certified traders face their own challenges as private-labellers and the major retailers' own-brand programmes pose serious competition for the alternative trade brands. What was the domain of small idealistic companies is increasingly dominated in the US by large brands and retailers and food service purveyors. Alternative traders are searching to define their role as fair trade continues to go mainstream.

TransFair USA also has direct competitors offering similar reform-oriented fair trade certification of a wide range of products. And the competitors do it without the political and marketing issues embedded in the complex TransFair approach of certifying, and creating markets and providing producer support. German-based Naturland and the Swiss-based Institute for Marketecology (IMO) have developed fair trade certifications using their organic certifying experience as a model.

In addition, certified fair trade products have a growing array of competitors doing social and environmental certifications. Utz, Rainforest Alliance, SCS and SA8000 are a few of the leading ones in the US. The labels tend to take even gentler reform approaches than TransFair and so often more easily win acceptance from corporate licensees. Their growth is slowed, however, by low consumer awareness.

The fair trade community in the US remains split in two main factions. Small and medium-sized alternative traders committed to change via new business models are squared off against certifiers and corporate retailers and brands that simply see fair trade as a route to be more socially responsible. Activists and many NGOs are caught between supporting the advances of fair trade while trying not to align their own identities with transnational corporations whom they typically don't support. The two visions of fair trade are stuck in an uneasy alliance.

For TransFair and the reformers, the playing field is big enough for everyone. They are struggling to figure out how to evolve their strategy to foster grassroots movement-building by supporting the emerging Fair Trade Towns campaign. They see movement-building as a key tactic to compete with the lower-standard certifications that are emerging. Given the uneasy relationship between TransFair and the alternative traders and NGOs, this will be a challenge that requires long term commitment.

The food alternative traders have a difficult challenge as well. Compared to conventional companies, they are less well capitalised, have fewer professional staff and are limited by their diseconomies of scale. Their desire to create fundamental change is tempered by their need to succeed within the current system. Their goal of supporting the market access needs of farmers and artisans has led them to support fair trade labelling for food products and soon, garments, even when the labels seem to favour the new corporate licensees.

The lack of a clear vision of how to differentiate a serious change agenda from the modest reform goals of the corporate fair traders is a serious obstacle for alternative traders. They have discussed – and some have tried – leaving the mainstreamed TransFair system but don't have a credible alternative certification or uncertified strategy.

Meanwhile, US craft-oriented importers, wholesalers and retailers have created two organisations to support their work over the years, the Fair Trade Federation and the Fair Trade Resource Network. These groups include some food traders but both are small and mainly involve craft products.

CONCLUSION

Bridging these gaps is a daunting task. Gulfs still divide reformers and transformers; craft and food traders; large and small companies; for-profits and nonprofits; and innovators and imitators. Yet all of these actors fit under the broad umbrella of fair trade. Finding a way to preserve the diversity of approach and forge a broad movement at the same time has eluded US fair traders so far.

The transformative alternative trade brands in the US continue to feel increasing pressure from corporate brands and look for new ways beyond TransFair certification to tell their stories. TransFair continues to adapt its change strategy. It is expanding the range of products it certifies, is going deeper into partnership with global corporations such as Starbucks and is supporting the Fair Trade Towns movement.

The competing theories of change appear poised to pursue increasingly divergent paths. How this plays out in the marketplace is the pressing question that is bedevilling many fair traders. The routes are unclear and the questions are many.

THE FUTURE?

The transformers and reformers are on paths to go their own ways. This will free up the alternative traders to create their own identity. But for many coffee and tea drinkers, banana eaters and chocolate lovers, this will likely add confusion and undermine fair trade. For the core fair trade audience, such diversity will provide meaningful choices to support beyond the increasingly mainstream TransFair approach. For NGOs, the terrain will be more difficult to navigate as they try to support the alternative traders and the certified corporations.

Farmers' organisations will also be caught between wanting to grow sales and supporting new models of business that are more aligned with poor farmers' values. As fair trade grows, the lack of a clear macroeconomic theory or vision of how all of these changes will lead to a better world will likely slow down major social transformation. They will continue to struggle to create honest conversation about power and fairness with the US fair traders – a difficult conversation to have.

Finally, as fair trade becomes more embedded in corporate America, alternative traders will begin to better link their work to climate change and efforts to lessen and eliminate poverty. If they are to survive, these small businesses will again become pioneers asking the difficult questions and forging new solutions.

NOTES

1. Carol Faulkner, 'The Root of the Evil: Free Produce and Radical Antislavery 1820–1860', *Journal of the Early Republic* 27(3), Fall 2007, pp. 377–405.
2. US LEAP website and personal correspondence, www.usleap.org, 2009–10.
3. TransFair USA, *Fair Trade Almanac 2009*, April 2010.
4. Ibid.
5. ICO website, www.ico.org, April 2010.

11
Tricky Waters

Tomy Mathew

I'm writing from Kerala where it is an unusually hot summer. Heat stroke, unheard of here until this year, has been reported from several places in the state. Fair Trade Alliance Kerala (FTAK), a farming organisation with a membership expected to produce a cashew yield of more than 2,000 metric tonnes, will struggle to meet its contractual obligations. For the second year running, the size of the crop will be half the expected harvest.

The reservoirs of our dams are turning into parched dry beds and the Kerala State Electricity Board, dependent as it is on hydroelectric power, is talking of an immediate 20 per cent power cut. We are still in March which, under normal conditions, should be a benign first month of the summer. Yet our coffee farmers in Wayanad waited with bated breath last week as a wild fire raged unabated in the adjacent forest for two full days. With vast tracts of one of the last havens of the Asiatic elephant reduced to ashes, we expect the hapless jumbos to stray on to our farmlands with far greater frequency and we are left wondering how great the conflict between man and animal will be this season. With an inflation rate nearing 20 per cent on the food grain prices, any yield loss in cash crops is fraught with dire implications for the food and nutritional security of very many farmers and their families.

'*Kaalavastha Vyathiyanam,*' our farmers say. This tongue twister is, for the average Keralite, common parlance for climate change. Interestingly this phrase is more Sanskrit than our mother tongue Malayalam, which could actually come up with half a dozen simpler and more straightforward words to describe the phenomenon. It is symptomatic of what happens when we are confronted with the unusual or the incomprehensible: we resort to the language of the priestly class, thus confining it to the realm of the esoteric.

While the science may be esoteric, the impact is not. It is real and felt. Intuitively we also understand that what we experience now gives just a taste of the potential future misery. Characteristically though, the science is being dealt with in the global north where the impact is going to be last and least. And the mitigation measures so far suggested tend to have both the smugness of these safe havens and also an irrational interpretation of cause and concomitant responsibility.

The smugness has been explained in part by two unique features of the unfolding climate change crisis, namely the unequal nature of the impact and the geographical separation of emission source from environmental consequence. As Mike Davis said in the *New Left Review*, '...global warming is not H.G. Wells's War of the Worlds, where invading Martians democratically annihilate humanity without class or ethnic distinction. Climate change instead will produce dramatically unequal impacts across regions and social classes, inflicting the greatest damage upon poor countries with the fewest resources for meaningful adaptation.'[1]

For all the positioning and posturing by myriad stakeholders in the climate change debate, there is little contestation about what has been emphasised by the UN Development Report of 2007–08: that global warming is above all a threat to the poor and the unborn, the two constituencies with little or no political voice.[2] Similarly there is near unanimity that the challenge of climate change cannot simply be met by limited practical steps advocated on television public service announcements. The reality is that what is needed is a determination to side-step the purely practical and to do the absolute necessary.

There is no mistaking the twin nature of the challenge that climate change presents:

1. A planet in peril calls for necessary and not just convenient mitigation measures. Now, convenience, in the context of our discussion, has this strange capability to couch itself in equity garb, against which we must be particularly vigilant.
2. Yet, all that we do must necessarily address the survival exigencies of those least equipped to adapt to climate change; it must be willing to look squarely in the eye the principle of cause and concomitant responsibility.

The temptation to invert the above order is best resisted.

But tempted if you are to draw a parallel to the above with the red–green debate of yore, it is certainly not far fetched. That debate unfortunately only led to entrenched positions and a stalemate of ideas which crippled decisive action. The burden of this piece is to explore if fair trade in principle and 'Fairtrade' in practice has the wherewithal to break the stalemate and propel us to action. Specifically, to our context, can global commodity trade in a climate challenged world chart a fair and green course?

But first things first and so a reckoning of what could be the implications of committing ourselves to doing what is necessary rather than what is expedient. Let us take on the Frequently Asked Questions of this debate, for it is important to make these discussions as direct, prosaic and close to home as possible:

Question: Can the world continue to trade commodities across continents in the volumes it does presently and still hope to save the planet?

Answer: No.

Question: Even if all of it was Fairtrade?

Answer: Irrespective.

Question: Can the planet survive if we continue to drink as much coffee, eat as much chocolate, or consume in myriad forms as much sugar as we presently do?

Answer: It cannot.

Question: What if all that coffee, chocolate and sugar were bought and sold on Fairtrade terms?

Answer: Irrespective.

So here it is in black and white – a voice from the global south; a voice from a producer hungry for more and more markets, who cannot stop complaining that Fairtrade sales are just not good enough. Above all, the voice from a producer who loves to hear Harry Hill's knitted character repeat a zillion times – 'Fairtrade works, what is the alternative? Unfair Trade!'[3]

The central issue is not transportation, as is often portrayed. Of course, the massive haulage of commodities across continents is unsustainable. Of course, the food mile advocates have a real case and are right in pressing for answers here and now. (Some of those answers have already come and what appeared to be extremely complex arithmetical juggling attempting to justify commerce with the third world has now solidified into incontrovertible evidence. The IIED's 'fair miles' formulation[4] will continue to inform the food miles debate in the future, reminding everyone of the crucial distinction between simple and simplistic conclusions on the environmental footprint of consumer choices. But that is beside the point.)

For in the hierarchy of problems the issue of food miles is lower down when compared to problems of food security, dwindling forest cover and endangered biodiversity in the producing origins. The countries of the south can ill afford to be cultivating cash crops for distant markets as they presently do if we are to still retain our optimism about saving the planet. But do we need more or less of fair trade in order to do this?

This is an excellent juncture to move from the dining tables and supermarket shelves of the West, which still retain an argumentative edge in the debate, to the farms and forests in the producing countries to see if another perspective emerges.

The Indian state of Kerala produces just under 20 per cent of its requirement of rice, which is its staple diet. This did not matter, until some years ago. The state's agriculture was encouraged to tilt heavily in favour of cash crops, for the country needed foreign exchange to fuel its developmental and industrialisation aspirations. We grew tea, coffee, spices, rubber, coconut, areca nut... practically everything that had takers in distant markets, but we grew little food for our own consumption. Central government allocations for the public distribution system (managing food at affordable prices), as a quid pro quo for our contribution to the foreign exchange reserves, and imports from the neighbouring states, kept us going. This was until our command (or planned) economy got dismantled, statutory rationing was withdrawn and the universal public distribution system in the state, which ensured essentials at affordable prices to the people, began struggling to keep itself afloat. The crash in prices of cash crops – we had not just the collapse of the coffee agreement but also the dismantling of the Eastern bloc to blame – was simultaneous. The perils of ignoring the food security of families and communities could not have come into sharper focus; but as anyone familiar with peasant life will tell you, there is no worse time to talk to farmers about food security concerns and the necessity of crop diversity as when the commodity price graph takes a nosedive.

Fair Trade Alliance Kerala, a small farmer organisation comprising around 3,600 farmers, was set up at the peak of this crisis. The guarantee of a minimum price for cashew, coffee, vanilla and other spices has brought in a small measure of predictability to farmers' lives. One of the first uses for the Fairtrade premium money we received was to fund a group farming effort by the farmers to grow rice and a community kitchen to prepare lunchtime meals for school children. Tubers – seasonal crops that significantly contribute to food security of farming households – have made a significant comeback. Delegates at the Global Assembly of the International Nut Producers' Cooperative / Liberation Foods, hosted by FTAK in 2008, were surprised that the agricultural exhibition, displayed on the sidelines of the event, included neither cashew, its flagship export commodity, nor any coffee or spices, which are the other products the farmers commit to the Fairtrade markets. Instead, the exhibition displayed about 60 indigenous varieties of rice, preserved in small but precious quantities by the farmers (this despite the relentless promotion of chemical fertiliser / pesticide guzzling, high yielding variety crops by the government). Also on display were at least two dozen tubers, innumerable varieties of bananas, various forgotten legumes and often ignored wild food. If ever evidence was needed about farmers fair-trading their way into food security, here it was.

COINACAPA is a Bolivian cooperative of brazil nut gatherers. Indigenous communities within Bolivia, Peru and Brazil hold the rights to gather the brazil nuts from the Amazon rainforests. The gatherers have formed themselves into cooperatives but negotiating the international markets has not been easy and most of the cooperatives are steeped in debt. The livelihoods of the gatherers hinge crucially on a remunerative price for brazil nuts, which means the announcement of Fairtrade minimum prices for brazil nuts could not have been more timely. In the absence of remunerative prices, not only will no-one undertake the risky and arduous task of nut collection, but also livelihood imperatives will override environmental concerns in people's approach to the surrounding forests.

Very soon after their first container of Fairtrade brazil nuts reached the UK (the gatherers having braved rains, flooding and landslides to achieve the safe transportation of the nuts across Bolivia, enabling them to reach the port for onward shipping to Europe), the cooperative along with eleven other nut producer co-ops from Asia, Africa and South and Central America, pioneered the formation of the International Nut Producers' Cooperative to take controlling stakes in Liberation Foods CIC, the world's first ethical nut company co-owned by producers. The 2007 annual general meeting of the cooperative took place following these momentous events. The focus of the AGM however was not prices, nor was it the debts the co-op was struggling to repay, nor the quality issues that fussy customers were always nitpicking about. 'The Brazil Nut tree is a patrimony to humanity,' the AGM declared. It must survive and the forests surrounding it must be protected for it to survive. Community strictures evolved about the stewardship of the forests that held the brazil nut tree. What hoards of punitive legislation had failed to do to prevent the deforestation in the Amazon region could be achieved by the Fairtrade guarantee of remunerative prices and fair market access. Even more, beyond their immediate stakes in the protection of the forests, the international solidarity that the Fairtrade supply chain engendered made the cooperative assert a true human connectedness. They were protecting humanity's patrimony, not just their own livelihoods.

An example this time from Africa. 'Fair Trade supports some of the most biodiverse farming systems in the world. When you visit a Fair Trade coffee grower's field, with the forest canopy overhead and the sound of migratory songbirds in the air, it feels like you're standing in the rainforest,' says Professor Miguel Altieri, leading expert and author on agroecology. But for the minimum guaranteed price, each coffee crisis would see a bit of that forest canopy disappear as the agrarian crisis in Kerala's coffee belt of Wayanad has shown. The coffee crisis changed Wayanad's landscape completely. Debt ridden farmers initially felled some shade trees and then increasingly 'clear felled' them. From the farms to the fringe forests was a short distance and the forest cover dwindled almost irretrievably.

Compare this scenario with the 'jumbo nuts' story FTAK talks about now. The man/animal conflict is nothing new in farmlands that adjoin forests. An entire crop can be wiped out by a herd of deer, wild boar or elephants. With elephants, it could be that your lifetime's toil can come to naught with perennial crops like coconut, jack, cashew or mango that have been around for decades. These can be suddenly uprooted by a marauding herd in the dead of night. Instances abound of farmers guarding their crop with lethal weapons, of elephants being killed or farmers being killed or injured themselves in attempting to save their crops. Some of FTAK's Fairtrade premium funds have been spent commissioning solar powered electric fencing around farms adjoining forest land – a benign deterrent to the elephant and round the year crop protection without sleepless nights for the farmers. Jumbo nuts normally referred to the large sized Indian cashews in the market. The Fairtrade cashews from FTAK are called 'Jumbo Nuts' because they are elephant friendly!

Continuing on the biodiversity angle: the Nilgiri biosphere in Kerala is a natural biodiversity hotspot and plans are afoot for the UN to declare it a World Heritage Site. The environmental sensitivity of farming operations here should therefore be a global concern. Apart from the cash crop estates of tea, coffee and rubber, the smallholder farming in the Nilgiri biosphere was characterised by crop diversity. The homestead farming traditions in this area acted to underpin its unique biodiversity and was also the basis for food security of households and communities. An average farm of one hectare grew at least 60 varieties of crops and on top of this were shade and wild trees which provided fodder and timber. The greenery they sport on a rain drenched monsoon day, to the untrained eye, will resemble a veritable rainforest. Next to deforestation, the shift to mono cropping is considered the most significant factor in the environmental devastation of the Nilgiri biosphere and the cause is clear: unstable prices and farmers being forced to change to crops which fetch better returns only to be bitterly disappointed by the time the new crop is fully grown and the prices crash. Coffee farms gave way to cocoa and rubber. Pepper gave way to vanilla and all to no avail. Today a Fairtrade farmer in the Nilgiri biosphere who sticks to homestead farming traditions can, with the support of an enterprising small farmer organisation, enjoy stable prices for coffee, a dozen tropical spices, coconut, cocoa, cashew and soon for rubber. There is no greater incentive this farmer needs to preserve the fragile ecosystem of the Nilgiri biosphere, one of the world's biodiversity hotspots.

Take the case of organic farming. That the environmental standards under Fairtrade, with its list of banned chemicals and sustainability criteria might mean some commodities should qualify as organic production is beside the point. Apologies if examples continue to spring to mind from near home but the parallels are universal. The farming crisis of the 1990s and first half of the present decade brought home the perils of chemical farming in Kerala. Spurred by grant funds, NGO programmes and government patronage, large scale conversion to organic farming took place in Kerala. The state was in fact first off the block in the country to announce an organic farming policy. The 'first world', we were told, is waiting for organic products – convert, certify and enjoy premium prices! Smallholder farmers formed themselves into collectives in order to comply with Internal Control Systems which enabled group certification. Certification agencies descended onto the scene amid a flurry of enthusiasm and a lot of meaningless frantic action ensued including farm diaries, input registers, and the irrational head count of every plant head. And then, nothing happened. No product got sold. All that enthusiasm dissolved into thin air. After a decade of such frenzied action on the organic front, what have we left to show? There are still organic farming organisations, the steadfast still continue. But almost all of them continue in business because they have had something to do with Fairtrade! I believe the viability of organic farming, the cause of sustainable agriculture, is best served under Fairtrade and it is not just what's happening on the supermarket shelves which is underscoring this point, but experience in the producing countries too.

So that is what you hear if you are 'listening to the grasshoppers'. Fair market access enables communities to trade themselves in to sustainable farming situations which give farmers and their families food security. At the same time it propels action towards community control over protection of natural resources. The global south therefore, needs more not less Fairtrade especially in a climate challenged world. In fact the disproportionate burden of climate change concerns that Fairtrade is asked to shoulder is a recognition of its spectacular success in effectively using the instrument of trade to address inequity and poverty compared to most other interventions. If you can do so much, you could do much more – this is what the food mile advocates, the slow food movement and the deep ecology activists are telling fair traders. And yet they are our allies. Contrary to popular belief, Fairtrade makes common cause with them. We, however, assert that our relationship with the planet is inextricably linked to our relationship with fellow human beings and this must be reorganised around concerns of justice and fairness.

One of the poignant moments of the 1972 United Nations Conference on the Human Environment in Stockholm is widely thought to be the declaration by Mrs Indira Gandhi, then Indian Prime Minister, that poverty is the world's biggest pollutant. Yet, the world has wasted around four decades since the dire warnings of Stockholm chasing the mirage of development as the grand panacea for poverty. Growth in its value-neutral form and of late in its 'inclusive' variant has been and is being chased with missionary zeal. Quantity of trade from the global south to the north has become part of the grand narrative of growth and development and is supported by massive governmental incentives and financial grants. It has made millionaires out of export license holders in the south, it has created sweatshops where thousands labour in inhuman conditions, and it has chemically abused vast tracts of arable land. What is intriguing is that the Stockholm conference, all those years ago, was acutely conscious of the equity angle of trade in addressing environmental issues. Principle 10 is explicit: 'For the developing countries, stability of prices and adequate earnings for primary commodities and raw materials are essential to environmental management, since economic factors as well as ecological processes must be taken into account.'

So you could not just trade your way out of poverty. In the absence of stability of prices and adequate earnings for primary raw materials, international trade would only perpetuate poverty and accelerate environmental degradation. Enter Fairtrade, dare we say…?

The logic of free trade is the Siamese twin to the conventional wisdom surrounding growth and development. Maximising efficiency and comparative advantage, the argument goes, will ensure that growth continues unabated and then the all too familiar 'trickle down' theory comes into effect, which is what the world's poor should see as their stake in the system. Fairtrade can now legitimately claim that it has effectively challenged this logic and this is the common ground we share with the environmental movement, even if we address it primarily from the equity and trade justice angle.

So, back to our dry Frequently Asked Questions. If the case is that global commodity trade cannot grow unabated, if it might need some stringent curtailing even as things stand now, then where do we begin? We must begin I suppose with those products that have minimal or negative impact on our optimal nutrition. And we must be comfortable in acknowledging the reality that the Fairtrade product basket as it stands today has quite a few such products.

But with issues of health, food miles, food security and biodiversity, all coalescing into that coffee bean, we tend to forget history. Coffee cultivation at the producing origins is unfortunately a colonial legacy and, characteristic of commodities with such legacy, a comparatively greater measure of injustice seems to have got embedded in the DNA of its global commerce. Fairtrade understandably did not mandate itself to trade in the feel good commodities of the environmentalists to start with, or even in commodities that contributed to optimal nutrition. It chose coffee where the injustice of trade was the highest.

So, how do we get rid of our caffeine addiction, for the sake of the planet? It must necessarily start with the world drinking far greater amounts of Fairtrade coffee than it does presently! Getting all that unfair coffee out of the way is our only hope for producing countries trading their way out of poverty, into food security, away from mono cropping and into sustainable farming and crop diversity. The world will produce and drink far less coffee as a result.

The challenge cannot be overemphasised: we need to find ways to ensure food security for everybody in a global population that seems destined to push past the 9 billion mark in the foreseeable future. And we need to have the planet in one piece to hold that population. If single-minded focus on growth is an untenable proposition, then our world henceforth will undoubtedly be one that is called upon to do 'more with less'. Distributive justice and sustainability will be critical elements of the commodity exchange of the future and Fairtrade is a small glimpse of what this might look like.

NOTES

1. Mike Davis, 'Who will Build the Ark?', *New Left Review* 61, January/February 2010.
2. UN Development Report 2007–08, http://hdr.undp.org
3. See www.chooseliberation.com/harry
4. *Fair Miles – Recharting the Food Miles Map*, IIED/Oxfam, 2009.

12
Scale without Compromise

Harriet Lamb

WHY SCALE MATTERS

The old former worker from the Chamraj tea estate in southern India was delighted. 'My sons used to argue about who had to look after me now I am old,' she said. 'Now, thanks to Fairtrade, I have a pension and they are fighting to have me stay with them!'

Mr Henriksen, the ebullient Fairtrade Coordinator on the estate, chuckles as he tells the story, but pauses to reflect on his sadness about the terrible position of retired people when money is desperately tight and they are treated as a burden. That's why he is so very proud of the pension scheme they introduced using the Fairtrade premium.

So this woman's story sounds like a shot in the arm. It is this kind of example of a direct change to an individual's life that drives people to buy Fairtrade, and drives campaigners to seek to grow the Fairtrade market.

Or is it? Mr Henriksen has a darker side to his story. Although the workers are spending every day picking the highest quality tea they are able, they are currently only managing to sell 10 per cent of the tea on Fairtrade terms.

So the premium pot is not growing fast enough. A difficult decision has to be made: it's decided the pension scheme will be suspended.

'You could say our investment in healthcare and the pension scheme worked too well,' smiles Mr Henriksen. 'Everyone was living longer and there wasn't enough premium coming in to top up the fund.' He has calculated that if they could only sell 30 per cent of their crop on Fairtrade terms, then they could roll out the pension scheme again, and finish the new secondary school they have been building – another project on hold. This is why he came over to Britain during Fairtrade Fortnight, indefatigably touring the country and calling on people to swap their cuppa to Fairtrade.

This is when the need to drive up the scale of Fairtrade really hits home. For years, Fairtrade tea bumped along at under 3 per cent of the UK market – that means only three out of every hundred cups of tea we drank were Fairtrade. This limits immediately the number of farmers and workers who can benefit. Today Fairtrade tea currently accounts for around 10 per cent of the UK market. It is an impressive rise in sales but it is still not enough – as the farmers are always quick to remind us.

In November 2009, I was, as executive director of the Fairtrade Foundation, at a meeting of the Network of Asian Producers in Chennai, southern India. One question kept coming to me time and time again: 'Why isn't the market growing faster?' We love Fairtrade, they kept saying, but we need to sell more of our crop on Fairtrade terms. In my ten years with Fairtrade, this has been a constant refrain.

On top of this, additional farming groups are queuing up all over Africa, Asia and Latin America to become Fairtrade certified. Yet they can only enter the system if a new market door opens – some sell the crops for which Fairtrade is famous like coffee; others have new ideas to extend Fairtrade for example to jute or rubber. These farmers are invisible. Campaigners don't meet them because their representatives don't get to come over here and address schools and public meetings. They don't get interviewed or photographed and placed in marketing and publicity materials. These are the farmers who are waiting to join a system that offers hope and empowerment. Globally some 2 billion people work hard for less than $2 a day, many – too many – of them growing our food and drink. That is why we need to scale up Fairtrade: across the nations of the world, crop by crop, community by community.

TEA – BREWING UP A FAIR DEAL

Tea is a good example of why scaling up is so important. Malawi is a small, landlocked state, sitting uncomfortably low in the world's ranking of poor countries. Poverty and HIV/AIDS take a terrible toll. Malawi is very dependent on exporting primary commodities sold too cheap to the West including tea, coffee, sugar, nuts and cotton.

On a trip to the south of the country, I met a tea smallholder, a proud and beautiful lady, who told me how little she earned for her crop, sold to a British company. She had five children and had adopted five orphans. More than anything, she wanted those kids to learn to read and write, opportunities she never had. But sometimes she had to take them out of school to put a main meal on the table at night. Sometimes she had to skip food to save the money to keep them in school.

When I met her, I knew we had to increase sales of Fairtrade tea. In Malawi, tea is the most important export and foreign exchange earner after tobacco. In India more than a million people are directly employed in the tea industry, with an estimated 10 million others earning their livelihood through the wider tea and ancillary industries. Rwanda produces just 0.5 per cent of the world's tea but this makes up 15 per cent of the country's exports. Ten per cent of the population of Kenya works in the tea sector.

The UK tea market is highly concentrated, with three global tea packers selling 60 per cent of our tea.[1] Tea producers, despite the care and attention they lavish on their crops, receive a much smaller percentage of the retail value of their tea than the traders and manufacturers. In fact, 40 per cent goes to processors, blenders, packagers and retailers which are based largely in richer countries.

Worse still, until the recent small upturn in prices following the financial crisis of 2008, producers were only receiving half of what they did financially 30 years ago. While tea prices have increased, the costs of inputs such as labour, fuel and fertiliser have gone up faster, thus reducing net income. Climate change is also having an impact with producers from India to Uganda reporting serious crop falls as the climate swings from unseasonable rains to droughts.

In fact, tea was one of the first Fairtrade products to hit our shelves in 1994. Over the past 15 years and more, Clipper, Cafédirect, Equal Exchange and Traidcraft, and a host of other companies have worked to build relationships with producers and bring quality products to Britain's tea drinkers. But overall, Fairtrade tea sales were just too small. We had to persuade more companies to commit to scale.

Marks & Spencer, Sainsbury's and the Co-operative have all risen to the challenge by converting all of their own label tea to Fairtrade and today that woman I met in Malawi is selling her tea as Fairtrade to Sainsbury's Red Label, one of the top five tea brands in the UK.

In total an estimated 750,000 people – farmers, workers and their families – are participating in Fairtrade through tea. On Satemwa tea estate, also in Malawi, there is increased paid maternity leave. Workers are receiving heavily subsidised mini solar panels saving them from buying the paraffin which used to use up a substantial part of their monthly expenditure. Boreholes are providing clean water to many more.

Perhaps most inspiring is the establishment of what is thought to be the largest adult education programme in Malawi, largely paid for by the Fairtrade premium and the Satemwa tea estate combined. There are 550 pupils aged between 18 and 80, of whom more than half are women. Classes are open to workers, spouses and near relatives and cover the primary curriculum plus English and life skills. Thanks to the solar panels the classes are able to run into the evening after work.

Seventy and 80 year olds are learning to read for the first time, workers are finishing the education they were denied as children, while parents say they are allowing their children to stay in school because they now truly understand its importance for themselves. Just one tea estate in just one country but an example which gives a real flavour of the potential within Fairtrade tea.

If thousands more producers are to participate, it needs the big boys to step up to the plate. But they are still undecided about coming onboard. One company boss told us the Fairtrade price and premium would take too much off his profits. Another told us that 'tea is a benign crop'. I do not think that they have ever met those women in Malawi.

NO COMPROMISE

Many companies considering Fairtrade want us, at the Fairtrade Foundation, to change the standards – and we do need constantly to change and improve our standards especially as we expand. In the early days we had different standards for each crop; then we understood the need to have generic standards on our core principles of organisation and democracy that are the same for all groups; then we improved our environmental standards. Now we are considering how to make our standards more accessible to producers and how to take into account the differences between, say, Asia and Latin America. Sometimes our minimum prices have been set too low, sometimes too high stifling growth. So it is a constant process of change as we learn and as we grow.

We focus on ensuring we have a rigorous, independent process to involve all the key parties in any discussions and decisions. Fairtrade standards are set internationally by Fairtrade Labelling Organizations International, which is jointly owned by the three producer networks across the continents and by the 23 labelling organisations including the Fairtrade Foundation. They consult with producers and traders, with independent experts providing the research which underpins it all. So, to the frustration of some companies, there is no way that Fairtrade standards can be changed just for one company in one country. This is why the public can trust the FAIRTRADE Mark.

I often say the very reason the public can trust the mark is that we trust no-one. We set the standards independently and we require evidence that the producers, traders and companies are meeting them, and when we find problems – as we inevitably do – we take action to address them.

TIPPING THE BALANCE

As we left the city chaos of Hyderabad, in southern India, I stuck my head out of the window to enjoy the hot air, heavy with the smells of the countryside with its ambling cows, dusty paths and scrubby bushes. A group of smallholders welcomed us into their small warehouse. They proudly displayed their immaculate record-books, noting who had harvested how much cotton. This was Zameen Organic, a new group which had only just sold its first harvest of cotton on Fairtrade terms. We moved to a ceremonial opening of the first purchase from the premium project. The brown paper package was cut open to reveal: a shiny set of digital scales. Intrigued, I asked why this had been their first priority. They explained that as smallholders, credit had been their biggest problem. Come annual harvest time, they would completely run out of money. Yet they needed to pay for workers to help with harvests. The banks shut their doors – smallholders were too big a risk. No-one wanted to lend to them. So they were forced into the hands of the local moneylender who charged a third again in interest rates and insisted they sold their cotton to him. And they knew he was cheating them by using rigged scales.

Now that the group is organised and can show its sales contracts with companies such as Epona, Hug and Pants to Poverty, it has obtained a bank loan. And those precious scales show that they, the farmers, are in control of their crop and their destiny. They know how much cotton they grow and what it's worth.

Across the world producer group after producer group have acquired sets of scales – sometimes huge industrial scales for weighing sacks of coffee or cocoa beans – each set a symbol of the farmers being in control. Indeed all are also a timeless symbol of the scales of justice which when it comes to trade we need to tip in favour of the farmers and workers.

This is why the Fairtrade Foundation's strategy for the future is called Tipping the Balance. We have a sense that momentum is building behind Fairtrade and that we have the tipping point within our sights: that if one big company commits to Fairtrade, then one by one others will follow and gradually a whole sector will shift to the benefit of the farmers.

Sugar is a sweet example of how this can work. For years sugar was the poor relation in Fairtrade, bumping along on the bottom with farmers selling tiny volumes. Then, after two years' work behind the scenes with farmers in Belize, Tate & Lyle announced in 2008 that all of its retail sugar would be Fairtrade certified. At a stroke, the farmers in Belize went from selling no Fairtrade to earning almost $4 million a year in premiums alone. It meant that Fairtrade sugar was suddenly widely available on the high street. Then, because Tate & Lyle could offer Fairtrade sugar in serious volumes, Cadbury's Dairy Milk could switch to Fairtrade using cocoa from Ghana and sugar from Belize. The success of this launch in the UK and Ireland was swiftly followed by the launch of Fairtrade Cadbury's Dairy Milk in Canada, Australia and New Zealand and Japan, followed by Cadbury's Chocolate Buttons becoming Fairtrade. The positive response triggered commitment to take the whole range of the Cadbury-owned

Green & Black's brand across the world. A second major chocolate manufacturer, Nestlé, also committed to Fairtrade certification and four-finger Kit Kats now proudly carry the mark. Before these confectionery giants had made their moves, Marks & Spencer, the Co-operative and Sainsbury's had decided that all of their own-label sugar should be Fairtrade. So by 2010, sugar is in the top three Fairtrade products in the UK and we are seeking out new smallholder groups to benefit from this transformation. Fairtrade's impact in the sector begins to become seriously significant – and the balance shifts further still as companies in other sectors track the success and consider how they too can come to the table.

In this way, Fairtrade can play its part in helping the international community pick up the pace on meeting the internationally agreed Millennium Development Goals which have halving extreme poverty in the world by 2015 as one of the eight targets. There is certainly a very long way to go to make trade fair. Two billion people – a third of humanity – work hard and struggle to survive on $2 a day or less, many millions of these involved in growing crops which we consume. Fairtrade is responding to this failure of conventional trade to deliver a better deal. It has shown that a fairer system of trade can work. The challenge now is to take this successful model and scale up the reach and impact of Fairtrade so that it can begin to truly transform trade in favour of the poor and disadvantaged.

USING SCALE FOR GOOD

Scale will enable the Fairtrade movement to deliver greater benefits. But it must also be underpinned by depth – so that we are benefiting the harder to reach smallholders in the poorest countries and regions of conflict.

CEO of Traidcraft, Paul Chandler has a clear vision of Fairtrade as a development tool. To him it is much more than just an ethical label committing big companies to supporting decent standards. It is also a vehicle which can reach out to those who don't have access to the market. He suggests that the major companies, perhaps working with dedicated Fairtrade organisations like his, could invest in more marginalised producers, buying from them and enabling them to get a step up the ladder. It is an idea being trialled in cosmetics in which companies have to show that they have a trading partnership with the producers, committing resources or sharing skills to support the producers in adding value. For example Boots, which had previously bought on the conventional commodity market, now has a direct relationship with producers in the Dominican Republic and is discussing future partnership projects with them that will add further value.

Ian Barney, managing director of Twin, the pioneering organisation which works with the producers behind dedicated brands from Divine to Liberation, believes the trick is to ensure that bigger companies engage with serious commitment, changing the way they work with producers:

I'm delighted that big players want to come into Fairtrade but we need to use this opportunity to ratchet up and improve the way they carry out their trade. How can their involvement in Fairtrade help to make coffee, for example, a more sustainable commodity? Within a commodity plan there might be a need to encourage sourcing from particular countries currently not having access to markets such as the Democratic Republic of the Congo. Part of the entry point into Fairtrade should be 'What are you doing currently on the ground and what are your aims going forward? How does this fit with a vision of a sustainable commodity strategy? How can we make the coffee sector in, say, the Congo a sustainable and valuable sector of its economy?

You, the big company, need the credibility that Fairtrade brings. We, in Fairtrade, need your scale and reach to transform sectors, especially in the most marginalised parts of the world, but it will mean changes in the way you do business.

Ian is not just speaking theoretically as Twin is already working with coffee farmers in Congo who already have an order from Sainsbury's.

Over at dried fruit specialists Tropical Wholefoods, the dynamic duo Adam Brett and Kate Sebag are brim-full of brave next steps for Fairtrade. They have worked for years with Mountain Fruits in the fragile border region of Pakistan, selling their apricots and walnuts in their own delicious bars and bags of fruit but wanted to increase their added value and income. Now they are supplying ingredients for Ben & Jerry's ice-cream; they are processing and selling the apricot 'kernels', the tiny nuts within apricot stones – and selling the stones to be ground and used in cosmetics including body butters in Boots. So absolutely nothing is wasted – great news for the planet and the farmers too.

Tropical Wholefoods' latest mission is to launch Fairtrade raisins from Afghanistan, perhaps a sign of Fairtrade helping to build the economic underpinning of peace. The most exciting breakthrough of 2009 was the launch of olive oil from Palestine with dedicated pioneers Equal Exchange and Zaytoun working with more than 265 farmers. It was a touching moment indeed to see farmer Mahmoud Issa finding the Fairtrade olive oil on a shelf in a Co-operative store in north London for the first time – a rare and inspiring moment of positive public visibility for Palestine.

The backdrop to the launch of four-finger Kit Kat was the experience of the cocoa farmers of Côte d'Ivoire, a fragile country beaten down by the ravages of a decade-long civil war. In 2008, half the population lived in poverty. There are shockingly high illiteracy rates of up to 95 per cent in the agricultural communities where the 6,000 farmers in the Kavokiva cocoa cooperative live. Their cocoa trees are old and yields low. Many of their children are not in school because there are none within ten miles. The nearest health centre can be as far as 200 miles away. Not surprisingly, when Kavokiva first sold its cocoa on Fairtrade terms its top priority was to invest in health and education. The farmers bought an ambulance to get people to hospital and opened a health centre which is estimated to have saved 30 lives in the first year alone. They built make-shift schools, set up bursaries and started adult education classes. But money was tight as sales of Fairtrade were pitifully low. Now, with growing demand for Fairtrade cocoa for chocolate bars such as Kit Kat they have the opportunity to sell as much of their cocoa on Fairtrade terms as they choose – which will transform how much the cooperative is able to invest in its communities and how much it can tackle persistent problems such as children working instead of going to school, as well as investing in improving productivity.

There is also a need to ensure that dedicated fair trade businesses survive and thrive as Fairtrade goes mainstream. Dedicated companies work hand in hand with producer groups, sometimes in the hardest places, painstakingly building up quality and quantity of crops until they can be part of a Fairtrade supply chain. Some, like Divine Chocolate, fruit company AgroFair and nut company Liberation are co-owned by the farmers, taking empowerment to a different level. When farmers are represented on the boards of the companies and at annual shareholders' meetings, this gives them a real say in how their harvest is sold and marketed all the way through the supply chain, as well as a slice of the profits when a dividend is paid.

In fact, Ian Barney from Twin suggests that all companies should have a commitment to meet and discuss key issues with farmers regularly:

> If we want to empower producers we need to look at ways farmers can be better informed about the markets they operate in, move up the value chain and gain a greater percentage of price than they currently do and a greater say in how companies trading their product are run. We need to find ways they can influence and have a voice in key policies which affect their lives, such as engaging with the local government in their own country so they can fight for their rights and capture greater resources to support their communities.

It is tough for these smaller companies to survive the commercial jungle, especially when multinationals are now offering Fairtrade and putting the weight of their marketing budgets behind them. One company was recently asked to pay £50,000 by an off-licence chain in order that they would agree to stock a new Fairtrade product. Such demands for payments, sometimes halfway through the year, are not uncommon but are well beyond the bank balances of smaller enterprises. So it is vital that the grassroots social movement continues to promote the dedicated companies who are also looking for the ways to tell their very special stories to the public. Some companies have teamed up with major brands, helping them source ingredients, or jointly market their products. For example, in Starbucks in the UK all of its chocolate is made by Divine while during Fairtrade Fortnight

2010, Ben & Jerry's ran a special marketing campaign jointly with companies including People Tree and Visionary Soap.

Paul Chandler says:

> Dedicated companies which understand Fairtrade will provide a bit of friction in the system and stop compromises being made. We are good at innovation and bringing new producers into the system. We can provide consultancy services to the big organisations. The need for the dedicated organisations depends on how well the large scale people start doing innovation and seeking a raising of standards: at the moment I don't think they do this.

This is a challenge well stated.

WINNING HEARTS AND MINDS

As the audience shivered under a flapping canvas tent at a green festival in Bristol, the questions started to get heated with one man questioning the involvement of major companies. Another man leapt to his feet, declaring himself a trade unionist and a councillor who supported Fairtrade because, he said, it is so democratic. Anyone and everyone can play their part in Fairtrade – whether they are watching their budget in Asda, or shopping for treats in Waitrose.

If increasing Fairtrade sales matters most to meet producer demand, it benefits shoppers too. Growth brings the economies of scale which help make Fairtrade more affordable and easier to find. Time and again, research shows that the public know about Fairtrade (nine out of ten people), recognise the FAIRTRADE Mark (seven out of ten), broadly understand and support the ideals of Fairtrade and would like to buy the products more regularly. So why don't they? Because, surveys show, they cannot find Fairtrade goods, or because they are too expensive, or their favourite brands don't do Fairtrade. Which is why it is such good news when major retailers and brands listen to that public demand and offer Fairtrade.

The outburst of public enthusiasm when Cadbury's Dairy Milk became Fairtrade blew me away. Catherine in Cardiff wrote: 'Can I just say this is possibly the best thing that has happened so far this year. When I heard, I texted all my friends. I am so happy I can finally think about eating my fave chocolate again. We nearly had a flipping party!' Letters poured into the Cadbury's team from schoolchildren and government ministers while the CEO's weighty postbag was livened up with sparkly purple 'Congratulations' cards. In New Zealand, anti-poverty campaigners even took flowers to the factory.

Major companies engaging at scale can help bring costs down. In addition, some retailers and manufacturers have also chosen to take the 'hit' and swallow the extra costs involved when they make the switch to Fairtrade. So your Starbucks Mocha Frappuccino or your Cadbury's Dairy Milk costs you no more. When Sainsbury's switched all of its bananas to Fairtrade, it did not increase the price even though this involved a significant financial investment in the first year alone. A move which puts Fairtrade within everyone's reach.

Some core supporters feel nervous that Fairtrade is working with some of the world's largest multinationals. However, when the Fairtrade Foundation commissioned a Globescan survey in 2010, asking people if their view of Fairtrade had changed from seeing it on household names such as Cadbury's and Tate & Lyle, more than 40 per cent saw such moves as a positive thing, with just 2–3 per cent taking a dim view. People said it was good that Fairtrade was being associated with big and well known brands and companies; that it showed Fairtrade is working, being accepted, is spreading and is helping producers and the poor. These companies can also bring more mainstream members of the public into Fairtrade, who will then of course try other Fairtrade products, while the dedicated core supporters and campaigners can keep putting the spotlight on the injustices in world trade and sink their teeth into the more weighty policy arguments.

The critics argue that Fairtrade should turn its back on multinationals whose broader practices do not make the ethical grade. However, the FAIRTRADE Mark was established as a product certification scheme to ensure, step by step, that producers get a better deal from trade. The Foundation is absolutely not a company endorsement scheme. We may not approve of everything a company does, but we do approve if everything which can be bought on Fairtrade terms in a product has been. And these Fairtrade terms are non-negotiable. In 2010, Ben & Jerry's announced that it was so nuts for Fairtrade that all of its ice-creams across the world would be Fairtrade. The company is of course part of global giant Unilever and Ben & Jerry's founder Ben Cohen is quick to champion social responsibility in his parent company too. Interviewed in *The Guardian*, he said the move to Fairtrade is 'certainly the best thing that Ben & Jerry has done since the acquisition. I think it is the harbinger that the day of first world corporations making huge profits off the exploitation of the third world is over.'

However it is vital that companies do engage with serious commitment. In the early days we had to accept that companies wanted to dip their toes in the ethical water – offering perhaps one small, special ethical line – to see if the public would buy the goods... Today, armed with the clear statistical evidence that people are putting their money where their mouth is, we encourage companies to take big, bold steps that demonstrate serious commitment.

Moreover, when companies put their backs behind Fairtrade, they get the payback. When Sainsbury's switched all of its bananas to Fairtrade, sales rose by 5 per cent, a significant rise in a category where there is traditionally very little market growth. If a shop is selling just one line of women's T-shirts made with Fairtrade cotton, that can easily get lost in a busy store. Customers are not on a treasure hunt for Fairtrade; as they rush round, maybe with bored or crying children they need to be able to find them with ease. But if a major chain declares, as Marks & Spencer did, that all of its main line of women's T-shirts are Fairtrade certified then the company can make this message highly visible with signs in store, in shop windows and with advertisements, PR and more. It's at that point that the public gives a company credit. Sales rise. Reputation rises. It works for us, it works for them and it oh so clearly works for the farmers. Then it becomes a sustainable and virtuous circle which can begin to make Fairtrade the norm.

On the other hand, if we do not reach scale, then we undermine the whole model. Companies will cheerfully turn to cheaper, lighter ways to give their goods an ethical glow without having to change their business practices. The public will wander off into supporting other causes, economists will claim that they always knew you could not intervene in trade, and Fairtrade will be consigned to a footnote in the history of corporate social responsibility – a sweet little idea that failed to take off and was only ever suited to the margins. No-one in Fairtrade is going to let that happen.

Rather, we are determined that over the coming years Fairtrade will be widely recognised as a beacon of good practice in trade and development, enabling the voice of the poorest to be heard at the highest level, opening opportunities for change and tipping the balance in favour of farmers and workers. In April 2010, a three year old race-horse won its maiden race at Newbury. Ridden by Jimmy Fortune, the horse was called Fair Trade. I am hoping it is a symbol: that all those producers and companies and citizens here are backing the winning horse – and, yes, it's called Fairtrade!

NOTE

1. Sanne van der Wal, *Sustainability Issues in the Tea Sector*, Stichting Onderzoek Multinationale Ondermemingen, 2008, p. 26.

13
Raising the Bar or Directing the Flood

Robin Murray

FROM ECONOMIC EXPERIMENT TO SOCIAL MOVEMENT

There is scarcely a corner of Britain which does not have an active presence in fair trade. In Keswick there are regular morning breakfasts of fair traders. On the borders you find fair trade goods in outby farmhouses. Co-op delivery wagons travel the motorways with 'Fairtrade' emblazoned in great letters on their sides. Schools, universities, and local government offices have become promoters of fair trade. In Lewisham borough council, the staff canteen has become a fair trade canteen, with pictures of farmers and their statements covering the walls. In less than a decade fair trade has changed from a practical experiment into a social movement.

What explains this extraordinary phenomenon, and how can this dynamic be sustained? In part it reflects a new kind of politics, one in which people are looking for ways to change things in practice and not merely express their views through conventional political channels. It represents a new social pragmatism. We know and engage with the world through small actions, but which have meaning because they are part of a much larger whole.

Just as the women's movement, in declaring that the personal is political, started the change in the household and everyday relationships, and in doing so created a new culture and social ethic, so fair trade is creating an ethic about how trade should be conducted, and providing a means for citizens in the northern hemisphere to relate tangibly to those marginalised by the world economy.

Initially it was seen as a micro economic project, a way of paying small farmers a better price for their product. It was a modest means of redistribution from the global north to the south. But with the growth of Fairtrade towns, of Fairtrade schools and universities, it has become a movement with wider claims. For some, like Britain's pioneer Fairtrade town, Garstang in Lancashire, it is nothing less than a movement to end the 'second slavery' that an unequally structured global market imposes on the poor.

The Quakers whose networks underpinned the campaign against the 'first slavery' led a boycott of sugar to strike at the economic interests of the slave trade. Fair trade has inverted this, replacing boycotts with buycotts. In a world now saturated by the media it has highlighted the negative by promoting the positive. In an economy of attention, a kitemark can be as potent as a strike.

The early fair trade companies and those running stalls after church or in village markets found their message amplified in the media, and further widened by the promotion of the initial fairly traded products. Consumer awareness of fair trade grew remarkably, those commercial companies closest to the consumer – supermarkets and coffee shops – were the first to seek the 'halo effect' of stocking fair trade goods, and their displays further widened awareness. Now even the mainstream brands are converting one or two of their products to Fairtrade, or in the case of the sugar giant Tate & Lyle, all their cane sugar. Sugar has re-entered the story, this time not in the shadow but in the light.

MARK TO MARKET

An expanded economy is also a more complex one. The pioneer brands – Cafédirect, Divine, Agrofair, Equal Exchange, Traidcraft and Liberation – surfed the wave of expansion. But in the past five years they have faced the challenge of all first movers. Competitors began to try to copy them, adopting the FAIRTRADE Mark, and seeking out supplies from approved producers. The supermarkets developed their 'own brand' Fairtrade lines. Now high street names like Cadbury, Nestlé and Starbucks are promoting fair trade in ways which mimic the pioneers. The song of the nightingale is getting lost in the noise of the dawn chorus.

The very success of fair trade now threatens these firms and their model of fair trade. They have always sought to operate a 'fair trade plus' model, that goes well beyond FLO's *Fairtrade* standards. They have all taken on a large measure of the risks of trade rather than pushing them back down to the primary producers. They have strengthened the position of primary producers in the supply chain, supporting them in developing their own warehousing and exporting capacity so that they can sidestep the previously powerful local merchants. Producers are joint owners of many of the fair trade companies in the north, participating in their governance, and taking a share of the profits. For them, fair trade – in the spirit of Garstang – has been a question of power and capacity as well as price. These Fairtrade companies now find themselves undercut by fair trade products that do not carry the costs of producer support, of participatory governance and the redistribution of risk.

The FAIRTRADE Mark faces similar pressures. It has been at the heart of the expansion of fair trade in the past decade. But it has its own competitors. Manufacturers and retailers who were unwilling to pay the price guarantees and credit conditions of the FAIRTRADE Mark, have supported a growing number of alternative marks – notably Rainforest Alliance and Utz Certified – or promoted their own ethical schemes. In Britain the vitality of the Fairtrade Foundation has meant that the FAIRTRADE Mark still predominates. But on the continent there are many countries where its sister labels now take second place to those which have lowered their standards to extend their coverage. Even in Britain potential new adopters of the mark press the Foundation to soften its standards. A kind of Gresham's Law threatens the economy of marks. There is always pressure for the bad marks to drive out the good.

In such a situation, the first task is maintaining the bar as the basis for raising and widening it.

THE RETAILERS

A key role in the future of fair trade is played by the retailers. There are two courses they can adopt. On the one hand they can play a conventional market role. They can treat Fairtrade products like any others, requiring key money to get on the shelves, and taking on the burden of high retailer margins to keep their place on them. They can encourage their buyers to source fair trade goods from anyone who conforms (or claims to conform) to the Fairtrade standards, treating its supply chains at arm's length without contracts or commitments. This approach will strengthen the downward pressure on standards and the mark. It will also maintain the current main anomaly of the fair trade supply chain, where retailers have margins of 35–60 per cent, dwarfing the proportion paid to the farmers.

The other course is to enter into developmental partnerships with producers and their associated companies in the north, using a retailer's pivotal position between consumers and producers to connect the two, to strengthen the supply chain by technical assistance, and ensure that there is a fair distribution of margins between producers and retailers.

One example of such collaboration is the Food Retail Industry Challenge Fund (FRICH) programme financed by the UK's Department for International Development. The programme part funds partnerships between producers, importers and retailers that develop primary producer capacity in Africa.[1] Such guaranteed access – once adequate quality and cost levels have been reached – provides some insulation from the normal day to day pressure on the retail buyers to drive down costs and maximise turnover.

Sainsbury's have shown their commitment to this second course by their decision to source all their bananas from Fairtrade sources. They have worked closely with the Windward Islands producers, providing a secure market (via a three year contract) in the face of low cost plantation competition from the three main banana multinationals in Latin America. They followed this up by Fairtrade sourcing 100 per cent of other own label products – cane sugar, tea, roast and ground coffee, and Kenyan roses, as well as establishing a £1 million Fair Development Fund administered by Comic Relief to promote supplier development.[2]

Then there is the Co-operative. The Co-op is the natural fit for fair trade. Just as in Italy there are regional cooperative supply chains selling through cooperative retailers, so in fair trade, retail co-ops are the final stage of a global cooperative supply chain. And the Co-operative Group has historically played a central role in the development of British fair trade. It was the first supermarket to convert its own lines to 100% Fairtrade (2002 for chocolate, and 2003 for coffee). It has been a long time supporter of a fair trade banana farm in Ghana, a banana cooperative in Costa Rica, and most recently a Panamanian banana cooperative which has been impoverished by a 'second slavery'-style long term contract with Chiquita.[3]

The Group is only one part of a larger archipelago of independent co-op retail societies, the top ten of which have a combined turnover of £3.3 billion. Most are members of the Co-op Retail Trading Group (CRTG), which although centralised allows independent co-ops to develop their own local or ethical sources which are then traded through the CRTG. All these co-ops could extend the number of 'twinned' partnerships with producers groups in the south. The partnerships should be formalised as an aspect of cooperative retail practice, and the buyers schooled in what is involved in fair trade supply chain relationships. Such practices go well beyond the Fairtrade standards because they involve technical support in improving production, processing and packaging as well as long term commitments to the partners.

For retailers following this second path, there should also be a transparent policy on margins. The French fair trade company Ethiquable has reached an agreement with the continental retail giant Carrefour to lower their margins on fair trade products to 25 per cent and this commitment is included on the packaging. UK retailers should now adopt a similar principle.

Another possibility would be to provide incentives on the shelves not just as price discounts to consumers – usually paid for by the fair trade suppliers – but extra premium payments to the producers. Modern smart cards, such as those used in the Lincoln and Chelmsford Co-ops, would allow the transfer of premiums to be itemised for every town and every customer, tracing it through to the producer co-ops at origin.[4]

CORPORATE PARTNERSHIPS

I am arguing here for a shift in retailer–supplier relations from one of dependent subordination to one of collaborative partnership. A similar partnership model relevant to fair trade has been developed by Muhammad Yunus, the founder of the Grameen Bank. He was approached by Franck Riboud, head of the French multinational Danone, who told him that he thought that large corporations could no longer ignore social issues, yet were strangers to the social economy. Riboud therefore asked him if he would work with Danone on a project to reduce poverty. Yunus agreed, but on one condition: that the project should be driven by its social and environmental imperatives not financial ones. That was the founding principle of the partnership. Grameen Danone Foods was established in Bangladesh as a social business, yielding no profit to Danone.

The two parties decided to make use of Danone's product specialism and produce a nutritionally fortified yoghurt that was cheap enough for the rural poor. Yunus insisted that rather than the normal centralised plant, they develop micro yoghurt factories that could be located near to the villages because it would mean less of a journey for the 'yoghurt ladies' from the villages who would do the selling. He also insisted that the containers should be biodegradable and edible. All these ran against the grain of the normal. But Yunus found that when pressed Danone had the capabilities to apply their know-how to produce radical socially oriented technical innovations. He has become a strong advocate of such social–private partnerships to harness modern technology for social goals.[5]

With the growth of environmental concerns, and with the expansion of fair trade to complex, manufactured products, such partnerships could become increasingly important. In rubber products for example, there is a need to develop the properties of smallholder latex so that it can compete effectively with petroleum-based synthetic rubbers, and to substitute dyes and other hazardous substances used in the production of latex-based products such as shoe soles or rubber gloves.[6]

As with the retailers, corporations ready to act in this way should have the producers' fair trade companies working as part of a joint team rather than as a subordinate supplier. It would be a way of raising the bar not just for individual projects but more generally by embedding fair trade practices within large corporations. There would be a case, indeed, for establishing an association of corporations ready to partner in this way. The Association would have its own supplementary codes of practice that would distinguish its members from the 'tick box' fair traders.

FAIR TRADE INNOVATION

Technical innovations of this sort are only one type of innovation relevant to the next phase of fair trade. There are organisational innovations – how to strengthen the management and governance of the first and second level producer co-ops, and the third level international co-ops and networks that have emerged as the result of fair trade.[7] Fair trade companies in the north need to develop mechanisms for closer collaboration. And there are supply chain innovations required with respect to traceability and the capacity to track fair trade products back to the farms and localities.

Advanced commercial logistics technologies would be valuable here. But there is also the question of processing flexibility that would permit short runs of products from specific villages and localities. NASFAM, the peanut cooperative in Malawi, has been working on its collection and quality control systems that now allow its peanuts to be identified down to a cluster of 12–20 farmers. Their challenge is how to maintain that degree of specificity through processing and packaging so that the consumer (and the quality controller) can identify these growers.

But there is also the question of new product development. It is a long process. Kuapa Kokoo in Ghana took five years to establish as a cooperative that was able to operate the collection and merchanting functions in Ghana. It took its branding company Divine a further four years to break even and expand. Cafédirect and Liberation Nuts had similar early life spans. Like trees, robust supply chains take time to grow.

Not all fair trade products are generated in this way. There are now over 3,000 products that have a FAIRTRADE Mark, many of these use materials and ingredients from established cooperatives, purchased on the fair trade commodity market. On the demand side, Britain is rich in the skills of product design and market testing to make desirable products. The challenge is on the supply side – issues of sustainable crop management, generic quality issues like aflatoxin in peanuts, new types of micro processing and strong producer cooperatives to manage all this. These all require producer oriented innovation.

The 3 FRICH programme linking retailers and primary producers, and the Fair Development Fund are important in this context, as are the initiatives of the Fairtrade Foundation and its parent body Fairtrade Labelling Organizations International (FLO). FLO has recently established a section that works with companies who have adopted the FAIRTRADE Mark, or are thinking of doing so, to identify the products they wish to convert to Fairtrade, and another group who search out and support suppliers who can meet the requirements of the northern markets. The Foundation is a promoter of innovation by its management of markets.

These initiatives could be greatly extended by adopting some of the methods that have emerged in the field of social innovation. They include:

- innovation camps that bring together different specialisms to work on rapid prototyping within a tight timeframe (from a weekend to three months)
- innovation scouts that scan the world for relevant technologies
- social innovators in residence who work within large corporations and small companies to look at feasible spin-off propositions

- social 'Silicon Valleys' or social industrial parks such as that being established in northern Spain in Bilbao
- launchpads that identify and incubate social innovations, with specialist advice and start-up funds
- competitions and prizes like Nesta's Big Green Challenge or the X prizes in the US, which pose problems (e.g. how to develop a low carbon public transit system in Chicago) and give large cash prizes for the best solutions
- open innovation platforms like Innocentive that connect those with problems to those ready to offer solutions.[8]

All these can be used to promote fair trade innovations, and could be hosted either by a small independent Fair Trade Innovation Lab, or by the Fairtrade Foundation itself.

Alongside the above, there needs to run a source of early stage innovation finance that is driven not by prospective financial rates of return (as with most venture capital) but by the goal of launching successful products and the deep tap roots that supply them. A Fair Trade Innovation Lab could be linked to a seed fund to finance prototypes and beta testing. Promising projects could be taken further through Community of Interest Companies (CICs). This company status has proved valuable for financing fair trade projects because it allows charitable funds to be channelled into start-up ventures (as in the case of Liberation) and maintains the fair trade mission as primary.[9]

A FAIR TRADE COLLEGE

I have discussed a number of economic mechanisms that can expand and enrich fair trade. But the development of a common culture of fair trade is even more important. Culture is a wide term. It covers festivals, language, performance, films, music and the many types of electronic media. In a sense it is what is at the core of life itself. There is scope for extending fair trade into such services and for establishing a network of fair trade cultural centres that could showcase these many forms of culture from the developing world, and provide a place where fair trade becomes more a way of life than a narrow economic transaction.

Here I want to focus on one particular cultural issue. It is how fair trade learns about itself and generates a common understanding. It is one of the features of successful civil economic movements that they develop their own structures of education. The British Co-operative movement, for example, established its own college in 1919 that developed successive generations of cooperative staff and managers. The retail co-ops all ran their own education programmes. The Mondragon cooperatives in Spain started from a training course and now have their own University. The remarkable Sekem project in Egypt, which has pioneered bio-dynamic farming and the conversion of 85 per cent of Egyptian cotton to organic production, has established its own Sekem Academy in Cairo. Such colleges are the source of vitality and renewal in any movement. Like a hidden attractor, they shape the patterns of activity and make coherent the disparate living centres that make up a movement of this kind.[10]

Fair trade lacks a college. Those engaged in it have not had a space to stand back and reflect. From the farmer right through to the importer and brander, the focus has been on the product, getting it from field to plate via a supermarket, in the right shape and at the right time. In the south, there has been some training in the running of cooperatives and in the business of trade. But in the north there has been almost nothing that is plugged into and informs practice. The new generation of fair traders has been formed on the job but without a wider context. Those in the commercial and cultural world who engage with fair trade – the buyers, the marketeers, the journalists, even the board members – have little substantive induction beyond the generalities of principle. Fair trade has been a movement of the hand and heart. It has not paid enough attention to the reflective head.

The intellectual challenge is this. Fair trade is not just business as usual conducted for an ethical end. It is a looking glass economy that, like Muhammad Yunus's Grameen Bank, discovers the limitations of the normal practice and reverses it. It partners with small farmers in marginal communities rather than large plantations. It shifts risk in the trading chain from the farmer to the importer. When world prices fall it raises the price it pays. It advances credit to those who have no collateral to give. It shares its ideas rather than hides them.

It is these reversals that have resonated with consumers and investors. For, like Grameen, they show that another kind of economy is possible. It is an economy of reciprocity, based around what we have in common rather than the antagonisms of the private market that keep us apart. Fair trade shares these features with other parts of the rapidly growing social economy. But the mechanisms and laws of such an economy are still too little understood.

This is where a college comes in. Its first task is to expand this understanding beyond the celebration of individuals and examples of ethics-in-practice. Adam Smith's theory of markets was more than a theory of entrepreneurs.

A second task is to develop a shared perspective and set of principles for operating successfully in this economy. For in this other kind of globalism, where the number of farmers scattered across continents, cultures and languages supplying Cafédirect is greater than the workforce of Ford or General Motors, a shared outlook is the binding necessary for such a dispersed movement to cohere.

A third task is to develop particular skills and methods that embody the principles of this different kind of economy. It is sometimes said that social business is 90 per cent conventional business and 10 per cent a social topping. In our experience the two should not be split apart in this way. Fair trade needs distinct management information systems, marketing approaches, HR policies, organisational structures – many shared with the most innovative firms in the wider economy. It needs its own type of business school.

Lastly the college needs to provide a space for those engaged in fair trade to take time out and reflect – what Donald Schon, the farsighted American management theorist, called 'reflective practice'.[11]

A college to carry out these tasks should be a college without walls and with many centres. It should be modelled on the Open University which was founded on the principle of people studying where they work and live, supported by local tutors, and fellow students, and gathering together annually. It was a model of decentralised and networked learning that shared many of the features of the great institutions of adult learning in twentieth century Britain, such as the education programmes of the Co-operative Retail Societies and the co-op inspired Workers Education Association whose tutors took themselves and their book boxes on the road.

The internet has allowed this principle of a decentralised college to grow exponentially. The Open University now has 180,000 students interacting with it from home. There are

16,000 conferences, 2,000 of them moderated by students, with 110,000 participants. Its student guidance website has 70,000 hits a week. This is a measure of the power of web-based education.

A Fair Trade College would link existing resources (in the Co-operative College in Manchester for example) with a multiplicity of study groups. Its principle would be that of the Open Source movement – the free posting of curricula and content on the web coupled with their constant upgrading in response to comments and submissions. The Fair Trade College would run some central courses – an action research degree for some, shorter courses for new buyers, or recruits to the companies. But much would be distributed, both for producer co-ops in the global south, and those wanting to engage with fair trade in the north. Such an Open College should become one of the main drivers of the next stage of fair trade.

EXTENDING THE SOCIAL MOVEMENT

In many ways the axis of the fair trade economy in Britain in 2010 has shifted from the complex architecture of markets to the gathering force of a social movement. It is this movement that will fuel the widening and deepening of fair trade. If we think of fair trade as a mix of philosophy, politics and economics, we can see that both the philosophy (in terms of the ethic of fair trade) and the politics (in the form of the Fairtrade towns, schools, and municipalities) have become key parts of its economics. The idea of the college is to develop the philosophy. What are the ways of sustaining and strengthening the social movement?

The growth phase has focused on products. Local groups have campaigned for shops and cafes to take fair trade goods. They became the local champions of the iconic fair trade brands owned by the small farmer co-ops. But a chocolate bar has its limits. It is direct relationships with the farmers that really matter. Fairtrade Fortnight has provided resources and a framework for connecting. Visiting farmers have travelled all over the UK, addressing meetings, appearing on local television, being welcomed in town halls. Occasionally the annual assemblies of the fair trade companies have led to memorable occasions – with fair trade fairs and dances. But for the most part fair trade activists have been separated from the producers.

In other countries consumers are more directly connected to producers. In Italy, the leading fair trade company Altermercato is part of a network of 500 One World cooperative shops. They are run largely by volunteers who engage with producers not just through the multiplicity of stories attached to the products on the shelves but through campaigns that emerge from these stories, such as the repression of the brazil nut producers in the Pando province of Bolivia, or the olive oil producers in Palestine.

Similarly in Japan, Altertrade, the fair trade company owned by and supplying the large consumer co-ops, organises regular exchanges between consumers who stay in the homes of small banana producers in the Philippines, and the farmers who return visits to the co-ops in Japan. Altertrade refers to this as 'people to people' trade, and as with Altermercato, it is direct trade between producers and consumers.

In Britain most fair trade is not direct. It is sold predominantly through mainstream retailers, sub-contracted category managers and private merchants. They are multiple curtains that stand in the way of the direct and continuous relationships that the fair trade movement needs if it is to sustain itself.

How to develop more direct links? Retailers could, like Altermercato, encourage groups of consumers to connect directly to their suppliers. This is most likely to happen through the British One World shops, or through Oxfam, and the online retailers (like Traidcraft and the Ethical Superstore) or through some of the Co-operative retailers.

The 100% fair traders and the Fairtrade Foundation could encourage twinning – of the kind that has begun with schools in England and Ghana, and which could be greatly extended between Fairtrade towns in the UK and villages in the global south. Twin Trading and its partners in the regions of Kilimanjaro in Tanzania, and Cusco in Peru, have launched a tourism project for visitors from the north to live among coffee farmers. There are initiatives to provide training and placements for members of southern cooperatives in the UK. There is also scope to greatly expand volunteering and technical support, and for all those involved, as in Japan, to speak about their experience when they return.

But it is to the web that we should turn for step change. As with education, the world of the web radically alters the conditions for connecting. To date most of the websites of fair trade companies have taken the old form, of content presented for passing readers. They have carried abbreviated stories and pictures about particular producers, and directory entries about producer organisations. But few have been interactive or have had the real time immediacy of Facebook or MySpace.[12]

With the growth of broadband and mobile phone technology, closer connections are on the horizon. What is needed is a platform that enables such interaction. Actively hosted, it would mean that Fairtrade products need no longer be merely a symbolic connection between consumers and producers, but a bridge connecting the two directly.

Across that bridge much could flow. There are few producer co-ops whose stories do not have a dramatic character, faced as they often are with the opposition of the local political and economic interests that they challenge. It is the detail of these stories that gives meaning to Fairtrade products in the shops, but that gets lost in the abbreviations of conventional marketing. The web is a medium that thrives on detail, on exchange and reciprocity, and the spread of the immediate. And it is a medium that allows the local to become global and transparent.

Such a hosted platform would best be established by a consortium of the 100% fair traders in conjunction with those active in the fair trade movement. In addition to facilitating north–south exchanges, and helping to spread an awareness of the conditions and activities of marginal farmers, its aim would also be to fuel the many new initiatives now being developed by fair trade activists in the north, such as the opening up of fair trade walking trails. Fair trade would no longer be merely a means for transferring small sums of money across the lengthy chains of international trade, but a platform for direct exchange and a common mobilisation. Fair trade now has the potential to enter fully into the information age.

THE PIONEERS

What role is there for the 100% fair traders in this next phase of fair trade? One course would be to accept the logic of the increasingly crowded fair trade market, and wind themselves up, their job done. Or like Ben & Jerry's, the Body Shop or Green & Black's, they could seek to work as an ethical implant within mainstream corporations.

Yet these companies remain key players in the wider agenda that I have set out. As producer owned companies, they are a principal conduit for producer engagement in the development of a fair trade web platform, a fair trade college, and the many fields of innovation. But to play this role the 100%ers need to radically change themselves from companies primarily focused on the development of particular products and services, to the hubs of wider networks.

On the one hand this means rationalising their own operations by merging their organisations or forming consortia to provide backroom services more cheaply. While in the initial phase it made sense to have separate companies, each with their own drive and identity, now they should consolidate, not least in marketing, to provide a stronger voice for the 'fair trade plus' model, and to develop their role as fair trade hubs.

On the other hand they need to turn outwards and actively connect to the potential partners in the new agenda – to the Fairtrade towns, the Fairtrade Foundation, to those with specialist skills, to sympathetic corporations, and to the environmental and cooperative movements. This means a shift in focus and governance from closed to open fair trade.

CONCLUSION

Social and environmental innovations like fair trade are often initiated by imaginative groups driven by a social cause. But the path of their growth has its pitfalls. If successful they can be absorbed and shackled by the mainstream, sometimes by the state (in the field of mental health for example) or by large players in the market. In recycling for example, large waste companies have crowded out the community innovators and lowered their standards. In organic food, US organic farmers have had to develop a new quality kitemark because the large corporate food producers used political pressure to water down the official organic standards. In both cases more has meant worse.

Fair trade need not go down this route. It controls its own standards. The governing body that sets the standards, the Fairtrade Foundation, represents many of the interests that want to enrich fair trade rather than dilute it. The FAIRTRADE Mark has its competitors, and faces its own pressures to relax the standards. But these are counterbalanced by the growing strength of the Fairtrade towns and of consumers at the checkout.

In this context the pioneers are far from done. They have an established place in the market and are seen as embodying fair trade's aspirations. They have much to live up to, both as standard bearers and innovators, and much still to do once their own economic position has been secured.

So the further diffusion of fair trade can be one of enriching its practices rather than reducing its standards. There are strong currents running in its favour. But to make the most of them the multiple springs of activity that have up to now followed their own courses, need to link more closely as partners to further a common programme of initiatives. The small rivers of fair trade that have already begun to reshape the contours of an impoverished economic landscape could together take on the force of a flood.

NOTES

1. Twin Trading, in conjunction with Sainsbury's, has accessed the FRICH fund to support coffee producers in Malawi and the Democratic Republic of the Congo. The latter's coffee has recently reached the shelves as a special 'coffee of origin'.

2. Sainsbury's is now represented on the board of the Fairtrade Foundation, alongside producers and NGOs.

3. There are examples of other multiples providing support of this kind. Marks & Spencer have launched a major ethical programme covering many elements of the supply chain. Their tea, coffee, sugar and conserves are all 100% fair trade, and they are rapidly growing the proportion of their cotton products sourced as fair trade. Tesco for their part have been a stable outlet for four years for fair trade brazil nuts by Liberation.

4. The Lincoln Co-op already rewards consumers at five times the normal dividend rate for those purchasing Fairtrade products.

5. Muhammad Yunus, *Creating a World Without Poverty: Social Business and the Future of Capitalism*, BBS Publications, 2007, chapters 6 and 7. One of the revelations of this process was that to the surprise of the plant engineers the micro factories turned out to be economic because the fact they were distributed not centralised meant that they could dispense with much of the expense of refrigeration, the yoghurt ladies using cooler bags on their regular runs to the villages.

6. Another example is in paper production, using renewable resources such as straw. The barrier here has been a solution to the problem of 'black liquor' produced during the processing of straw. Its pollution is causing much of the rice straw production in India and China to be closed down, with resulting pressure on virgin forests and a rise in imported waste paper. The UK social company Bio Regional has been working for more than a decade in partnership with commercial paper companies to find a solution to this problem, and then diffuse the know-how cheaply. It represents a form of fair trade in reverse, and has echoes of the fair procurement that was an initial driver of fair trade companies like Twin Trading.

7. It is one of the achievements of the last decade that there are now international producer co-ops that play an active role in

fair trade governance in coffee and tea (CPL), fresh fruit (CPAF), nuts (INPC), and in FLO and the Fairtrade Foundation itself. The organisational challenge is how to use the web and modern technology like telepresence to lower the cost and extend the range of communication between the members of these international co-ops and their companies in the north.

8. For an initial mapping of methods of social innovation see Robin Murray, Julie Caulier-Grice and Geoff Mulgan, *The Open Book of Social Innovation*, Nesta 2010, and the website www.socialinnovator.info

9. CICs have their own regulator, and CIC companies are required to submit an annual report showing how their work has helped their 'community of benefit' and realised their mission.

10. The University of Gastronomic Sciences in Pollenzo and Colorno in northern Italy was established as a primary catalyst for the international slow food movement, which saw a shared culture and intelligence as an alternative to any attempt to centrally police a 'slow food' brand. See Carlo Petrini, *Slow Food Revolution*, Rizzoli International, 2006, and Geoff Andrews, *The Slow Food Story*, Pluto Press, 2008.

11. Donald Schon, *The Reflective Practitioner: How Professionals Think in Action*, Basic Books, 1983.

12. Divine is a partial exception, particularly their Dubble website (www.dubble.co.uk) connecting young people in Britain and Ghana.

14
Conclusion
When the Rain Stops

John Bowes

In his classic novel, *One Hundred Years of Solitude*, Gabriel Garcia Marquez refers to an historical event which took place in December 1928. 'Gabo' was just 20 months old when 30,000 Colombian banana workers went on strike for better pay and working conditions. The Colombian army, after its officers had allegedly been lavishly entertained by the United Fruit Company, opened fire on more than 3,000 workers occupying the main square in Cienaga. Nobody knows for sure how many died; perhaps as many as 1,000 poverty-stricken banana workers breathed their last on the single most controversial day in Colombian history.[1] This tragic incident etched deep in the memory of the young Marquez. In his fictional version of events the massacre in the square was followed by an organised cover-up; the corpses of the victims were freighted seaward to eliminate any evidence of the tragedy; the strike ended, and the banana company agreed to the workers' scaled-down demands, which were to be implemented 'when the rain stops'.[2] But the rain didn't stop. It rained for four years, eleven months, and two days.

And by the time the deluge had ended the banana company had upped-sticks and left the community in ruins.[3]

Marquez's outstanding novel reflects the history of South America; his fictional version of the tragedy at Cienaga mirrors the trading relationship between the north and the south; the economic power of the multinational companies in the United States being savagely and ruthlessly used to exploit the people and nations on the south of the American land mass. A situation not unique to the American continents but also demonstrated on a global basis as the trading patterns established in the eighteenth and nineteenth centuries, often with the aid of force and violence, still conspire to benefit the nations in the northern hemisphere at the expense of the peoples in the south. A process which has left half of the world in poverty; with countless millions hungry, desperate, and without hope.

It is this imbalance in the trading system that fair trade is designed to address by persuading consumers in the north to pay a little more for some basic commodities so that a fairer share of the benefits can help realise better lives for the farmers and workers whose back-breaking toil nurtures produce from the hard earth. It has achieved a remarkable degree of success. The FAIRTRADE Mark is now firmly established as the world's leading ethical label. More than 70 per cent of people in the UK now recognise the mark and the public believe that supporting fair trade is the most effective way for them to play a part in tackling poverty.

Critically, it has helped change the lives of millions of people in the developing world. There are now 879 producer organisations in 58 developing countries participating in Fairtrade. They benefit from guaranteed minimum prices and collectively earn more than €40 million every year from Fairtrade premiums. Over 7 million people currently have the opportunity to enhance their lives, not only as a result of the financial benefits which flow from fair trade, but also through the vital sense of empowerment offered by democratic participation in the process. They have a better share of the trading benefits and also a little more control over their own lives and futures.

But this progress has not been achieved without difficulties. The concept of fair trade could hardly be simpler but the task of delivering it on the ground has all manner of complexities. The bureaucracy which must inevitably accompany a global auditing system is expensive, time consuming and frustrating but, at the same time, is critical in delivering customer confidence in the FAIRTRADE Mark. In Ghana and Côte d'Ivoire, where the cocoa trade is dominated by thousands of small farmers, the sheer complexity of the business has presented a major challenge for the successful application of certification and auditing procedures. The foundation and development of El Guabo in Ecuador, now a cooperative of more than 460 farmers, has demonstrated the importance of careful 'political' management, and the critical role that inspired individuals can play, as well as the obvious predominance of economic and financial criteria, in order to achieve sustained success.

While the success of the FAIRTRADE Mark has been practically unrivalled by other 'ethical' labels in the UK it has, nevertheless, started to face some 'competition' from the Rainforest Alliance. On the basis that some ethical commitment is better then no ethical commitment we should perhaps welcome this development. But it is important to realise that the Rainforest Alliance focus appears to be primarily on environmental conservation; it doesn't offer farmers a guaranteed price or do anything to replicate the Fairtrade premium. As the focus of fair trade is so clearly about alleviating poverty, and building sustainable trading relationships, it is sometimes forgotten that carrying the FAIRTRADE Mark also requires producers to limit their impact on the natural environment by making environmental protection an integral part of farm management. Nevertheless, there is a real concern that some major companies will cheerfully turn to cheaper, lighter ways to give their brands and products an ethical glow without having to make any material change to their business practices.

But environmental issues offer even bigger challenges to fair trade. The very nature of the project involves transporting commodities across the world; burning carbon and contributing to global warming. No matter that the international transportation of Fairtrade products to the UK accounts for only 0.001 per cent of our carbon emissions, the concept of food miles, together with recycling and energy efficiency, are easy to understand and have been grasped by millions as the obvious issues to address in the search for a simple panacea for the climate crisis.[4] Shopping for locally produced products, recycling household rubbish and turning the television off standby may be practical ways for individuals to make a small contribution but they will not solve the greatest crisis that human kind has ever faced. The problems are of an altogether different scale.

Climate change is predominantly the result of excessive carbon emissions by the rich nations in the north – annual carbon emissions per person are 172kg in Bangladesh compared with 9,000kg in the UK and 21,000kg in the US.[5] In this it mirrors trade in the sense that the affluent have the benefit of high levels of energy utilisation but the impact is global; there is a geographical separation of the emission source from the environmental impact. Global warming is above all a threat to the poor and the unborn. They have no part in the scientific debate taking place in the relatively safe havens of the northern hemisphere where the full impact of the predicted devastation is likely to be felt last. The temptation for policy makers and politicians is to address the issue in ways which are palatable and convenient when what is required is radical action to address the central issues. They need to do what is necessary rather than what is convenient.

Much of the focus has been on transportation, and there must be an issue about the long term viability of commodity trading in luxury rather than necessary items, but the immediate and central issues are about food security, dwindling forest cover and endangered biodiversity. Many of the problems are as a result of a world trading system which has encouraged the focus on mono crops in the developing world. This, in turn, has indirectly encouraged deforestation and farming methods which damage biodiversity. In this context, fair trade potentially offers an environment lifeline. The guarantee of fair prices and market access can act to support farming communities without the need for clearing forest. Fair trade arguably supports some of the most biodiverse farming systems in the world and fair market access has enabled communities to trade themselves into sustainable farming situations and food security.

The United States of America is the largest consumer market on Earth. No other country on the planet could do more to address the climate problem and establish a fairer trading system. While fair trade has experienced strong growth in the States, which in absolute terms is the largest single market for fair trade products, overall market penetration is low.

Yet, if we are to have a true revolution in trading practices it is difficult to see how it can be achieved without the US fully on board. This represents the greatest single challenge for fair trade campaigners in the north.

Whilst the focus should be on persuading the American consumer of the case for fair trade, a prerequisite for success in the US appears to be some kind of accommodation between the two divergent wings of its fair trade 'industry'. The debate is split into the transformer view, associated with alternative trading organisations, and the reformer view, associated with fair trade labelling. The transformers have the more radical approach and want to transform the trading system by creating non-corporate partnerships linking the farmer to the consumer. The reformers have a more incremental approach and essentially seek to operate within established trading frameworks. In this context, they have been happy to conclude deals with major multinational companies such as Starbucks and Dole, organisations which many in the fair trade movement have historically associated with some of the worst abuses that their current efforts are designed to address. This discomfort is not exclusive to northern activists; many in the south feel the same way. The involvement of these companies, and others like Nestlé, Walmart and Tesco, is seen by some of the pioneers in the southern hemisphere as a betrayal of first principles.

These concerns are also shared by many in the UK. When Nestlé incorporated the FAIRTRADE Mark onto its Partners' Blend coffee there were plenty of dissenting voices who saw it as a grotesque act of cynicism and a betrayal of the cause. And many still hold such views but in the UK the emphasis has been on partnership and cooperation. Too much introspection seems an extravagant and self-indulgent luxury when so many in the developing world are suffering the inequities of an unjust trading system. From the very outset the fair trade campaigners in Garstang, Lancashire, recognised the FAIRTRADE Mark as the best vehicle for bringing the alternative trading system into the mainstream. Their campaign, and the Fairtrade Towns initiative which followed in its wake, focused on promoting awareness and recognition of the FAIRTRADE Mark. These pioneer activists believed that the greater the sales of products carrying the mark, the greater the impact on the livelihoods of producers. And whilst alternative traders like Twin developed specific brands like Divine, Liberation and Cafédirect, they have always actively supported the Fairtrade Foundation and the FAIRTRADE Mark. This essential unity of purpose has allowed the Fairtrade Foundation to provide strong and powerful leadership for the UK movement.

The Fairtrade Foundation's emphasis has been on delivering scale without compromising on standards. This strategy has inevitably involved them in working with all of the major supermarket groups and some major multinational manufacturing businesses. The Foundation understands that some of its core supporters feel uncomfortable with this but reason that they are only a small minority. Clearly, if the movement wants to have a serious impact on addressing poverty in the developing world it has to persuade some of the big beasts in the trading jungle to change their practices and elect to support Fairtrade. Any other approach would condemn the project to irrelevance and obscurity.

The Foundation has been remarkably successful at bringing many large businesses some way into the fold. This is not a simple process. For most businesses it is counterintuitive to elect to pay more for their products. Modern British retailers are programmed to deliver ever-increasing sales and profitability in a market which is increasingly competitive. To ask them to increase their prices or reduce their margins simply goes against the grain. Hence, in the early days, it is perhaps no surprise that many of them were reluctant to take the plunge. The Co-op was the first major retailer to seriously engage with fair trade and, as a result, deserves a special place in the movement's history. But they are a membership-based organisation with a set of ethical values closely aligned to fair trade. Other retailers were always going to be more difficult to bring on board.

There is a tendency to view large organisations as a single entity with a single dominant personality. In fact these businesses are in a slow and sometimes hardly discernible perpetual flux in response to changing market conditions and internal management changes. This is most easily seen when a new chief executive takes up the reins and redirects the business, resulting in changes in strategy and the allocation of power between different functions in the business. A retail business is much more likely to engage with fair trade when its strategy is market led and the marketing function is high profile within the organisation; conversely it is less likely to make ethical value-based changes when the finance or operational functions hold the upper hand.

Nor should we understate the importance of committed individuals. In El Guabo, Jorge Ramirez used his personal charm and charisma to inspire the local farmers. Bruce Crowther was the inspiration for the Garstang pioneers. At the Co-operative Group it was a small cadre of committed managers who kick-started their responsible retailing revolution. And in Sainsbury's it was one tenacious and resilient individual who, from a modest place in the management hierarchy, effectively delivered what is arguably the single most commercially important Fairtrade decision that has yet been made; a decision that was 'assisted' by a perspicacious chief executive, an accident of circumstance, and just a little alcohol.

Senior executives and buyers in large retailers have an enormous amount of power – perhaps much more than they realise. With a single stroke of the pen, or a click on a mouse, they can achieve in a second what might take a group of activists a lifetime to deliver. It is vital to engage with these people, and convince them of both the moral and commercial case for fair trade, because, taken collectively, they have the power to change the lives of millions of the poorest people on the planet.

As an increasing number of large businesses start to support Fairtrade this inevitably puts pressure on the specialist businesses that have played such an important role in the development of the project. As manufacturers and retailers recognise the importance of fair trade, and the potential for scale, they increasingly seek to source product directly rather than through the alternative trading organisations or their brands. This is an experience shared on both sides of the Atlantic Ocean and presents a real dilemma for these specialist businesses. As their volumes and margins are squeezed it begs the question as to whether, after setting up the initial supply chains and creating the initial markets, they have now fulfilled their role in the project. They have given fair trade the foothold it needed but, having sown the seed and seen it flourish, the reward for their impressive success may ultimately be obsolescence. But with fair trade still in its infancy it would seem somewhat premature to consign these pioneering organisations to history. They need a clear vision of how to differentiate themselves.

Their task is to establish a new paradigm; to extend the scope and raise the bar for fair trade. Businesses like Divine, AgroFair and Liberation are all part-owned by their producer partners; they have created integrated fair trade supply chains with the farmers democratically empowered with seats in the boardroom. This level of producer involvement should be of interest to customers who take ethical issues particularly seriously, but relatively few will be aware of the distinction, and the appeal will always be to a minority. These businesses simply need to go further and faster. They need to offer something materially different to the essentially commoditised approach of the large manufacturers and retailers. They could, for instance, publicly commit to pay more for the product. The Fairtrade price is essentially a safety net which is set at a level sufficient to cover the cost of sustainable production. The farmers and workers still have a tough existence. Therefore, committing to pay at a level greater than the Fairtrade price is a legitimate means of generating a greater level of wealth transference by putting more money back into the developing world. Undertaking more of the processing in the south rather than the north is another way of ensuring that the needy have the opportunity to take a greater slice of the supply benefits.

There are obviously cost implications associated with this type of initiative and the specialist businesses need to be certain that they have good access to the market. What has been referred to as Fairtrade Plus will appeal to the most seriously ethically committed but it is likely to be a niche market accounting for no more than 5 per cent of customers. The major UK retailers have been exercising tight control over their inventories during the recession and some Fairtrade brands have found it difficult to stay on the shelves. Gaining commitment to new or extended listings would be a considerable challenge. But specialist organisations have a strong card to play. They are good on innovation and have an unchallenged expertise in establishing fair trade supply chains. They also have an unrivalled credibility in terms of their integrity and ethical credentials. For retailers who seek to differentiate themselves on an ethical platform they potentially represent a rich source of knowledge and expertise on which to help build a unique positioning.

Retailers like the Co-op and Sainsbury's have invested in Fairtrade. Whether their motivation has been about values or branding they obviously value the credence and kudos that leadership of the ethical agenda can offer them. Staying ahead of the game is a real challenge for these businesses. Is it credible to think that a major retailer might publicly commit to converting their entire own brand range to Fairtrade; to ensure that everything that can be Fairtrade sourced will be Fairtrade sourced?

This would be a great step forward but the next key paradigm shift, for businesses which genuinely want to lead the ethical agenda, might be a change of emphasis from conventional market trading to development partnerships with producers and specialist fair trade businesses in the north, to strengthen the supply chains so critical to producers, and ensure a fairer distribution of margins.

For the specialist businesses an evolution of this kind could open up important new opportunities. They would need to shift from their current exclusive focus on products and brands to develop a new role as the hub for a wide network of services focused on innovation, communication, and education. It could be an opportunity for re-engaging with their pioneering roots, pushing the boundaries for others to follow, and providing a real stimulus for the fair trade revolution.

Many activists are uncomfortable with the entry of the large multinational brands. They fear that the big corporations will crush the alternative traders and their vision of change. The World Fair Trade Organization, the trade association of alternative traders, is preparing to introduce its own certification of whole organisations; this approach requires that all products traded by a company must be fairly traded. In contrast, the Fairtrade Foundation in the UK argue that the FAIRTRADE Mark was established as a product certification scheme to ensure, step by step, that producers get a better deal from trade. It is not, in other words, a company endorsement scheme. But there is a real issue here which was demonstrated in 2007 when Pratts, a banana ripener and distributor, a Fairtrade licensee, and a supplier to a number of major retailers, was found to be exploiting migrant workers at its packing station. The media inevitably sought to use the story to undermine the credibility of Fairtrade, which clearly illustrates how the wayward behaviour of any element in the supply chain might have an adverse impact on the project and its reputation. Conversely, it also suggests that there is an implicit expectation in some quarters that only a holistic discipline along the entirety of the chain can guarantee a truly ethical proposition.

What emerges from this thinking is an essential duality. Is it possible to conceive of a two tier proposition? Could the divergent thinking within the fair trade 'industry' polarise into two distinct offers? The first geared to scale based on existing criteria and the second focused on a greater level of empowerment and wealth transference, and a holistic approach to the entire supply chain. Could this polarisation be at some stage formalised in a way which strengthens the leadership which has been so critical to the success experienced in recent years?

Whilst these debates engage us the world moves on. One of the most important developments in recent years has been the growth of fair trade between nations in the southern hemisphere. The Bolivarian Alliance for Peoples of the Americas (ALBA) now has ten member nations and is focused on developing the potential for fair trade on a local and south–south basis. In a short time it has achieved a great deal of success and is illustrative of the potential that exists for securing trade justice between the nations in the south. It is too easy to see the success of fair trade as a northern movement. Much of what has been achieved so far has been based on the courageous and visionary leadership of producers in the south. In Nicaragua it was the Sandinista revolution, and the land reform which followed in its wake, that kick-started the development of cooperatives and their own inexorable journey towards fair trade. Over 30 years later they still proudly refer to revolution and about striving to contribute to a better world through concrete actions.

Fair trade has certainly strived to improve the world and no-one could accuse the movement of inaction. But despite all the self-evident success, can we seriously talk about a Fair Trade revolution? In the UK it still accounts for less than 1 per cent of the total UK grocery market. Although almost all of the supermarkets stock Fairtrade products only one or two of them have put serious marketing investment behind the concept. Some major brands have elected to support Fairtrade but the majority are still sat on the sidelines, some having opted for alternative green or ethical badges as cheaper and less demanding alternatives. But fair trade has won a battle of ideas; it has achieved a revolution in the mind.

An astonishing nine out of ten people in the UK recognise the FAIRTRADE Mark and seven out of ten broadly understand the concept and support its ideals. This is an amazing level of brand recognition and reflects almost universal support for the Fairtrade concept. To achieve this in a little over a decade represents a fundamental paradigm shift in terms of how people think about their ability to have some influence on problems in the developing world. It represents a remarkable change in customer consciousness, a revolution in the way people think. Fair trade has won the hearts and minds of the British people; the challenge now is to turn that overwhelming support and goodwill into Fairtrade sales.

In *One Hundred Years of Solitude* Macondo, the fictional village at the heart of the novel, was left in ruins when the banana company left. When the rain finally stopped the community was occupied by unemployed and angry people who were tormented by the prospect and bitterness of a static present.[6] This is a dark vision; a vision shorn of hope.

The non-fictional reality is certainly desperate. In August 2008 I visited a small and remote community of indigenous Indians in Panama. I visited a lady who had ten children. Her husband, sick of the poor rewards for backbreaking labour on the banana plantation, had left home some time previously to try to find work in Panama City. She didn't know when he would be back and had no practical means for communicating with him. So she was on her own trying to bring up a large family on a diet that consisted mainly of bananas and root vegetables. Her home was a wooden construction built on stilts. When I climbed the stairs to meet her and her children I was struck by how amazingly tidy it was but then, of course, she had virtually no material possessions. The place was full of neatly stored hammocks, varying greatly in size, which represented the children's sleeping arrangements. I was admiring the ingenuity of all of this when, in the cramped space, I almost bumped into a string bag which was hanging from the ceiling in the middle of the room. At first I was annoyed at my own clumsiness, and then alarmed when I realised what was inside: the bag was a cot for a one month old baby. As I recovered from this modest shock I realised that there was another child at my feet – a two year old little girl was laid out sleeping on the wooden floor. She was clearly distressed by a quite severe asthmatic condition and was struggling with her breathing. Her mother did not have the ten dollars required to pay for her medication. We did the obvious thing. We took mother and child to a medical centre and paid for her medicine. What else could we do?

The area is dominated by one of the great multinational banana companies and this community is on the site of an old banana plantation. The water table is high (it rains a lot) and so the well, a tin drum, was full almost to the surface. Unfortunately the land had been subjected to decades of spraying when it was being worked and so the water is contaminated by the pesticides embedded in the earth.

But unlike the fictional Macondo there is hope. On my visit I was accompanied by the marketing director for the Co-op's food business and they subsequently began sourcing Fairtrade bananas from the Coobana cooperative in April 2010. This will give the local farmers and workers the opportunity to earn a little more for their efforts and wrest a greater level of control over their own lives. This is what fair trade can deliver; the prospect of a brighter future for the downtrodden and the impoverished. Which all goes to show that the world can change for the better. Good things do happen.

NOTES

1. Gerald Martin, *Gabriel Garcia Marquez: A Life*, Bloomsbury, 2008, pp. 40–3. See also Peter Chapman, *Bananas: How the United Fruit Company Shaped the World*, Canongate, 2007, pp. 89–93.
2. Gabriel Garcia Marquez, *One Hundred Years of Solitude*, Everyman's Library, 1998, pp. 300–13.
3. Ibid., pp. 314–30.
4. Fairtrade Foundation estimate.
5. Fairtrade Foundation estimate.
6. Gabriel Garcia Marquez, *Leaf Storm*, Penguin Books, 2008, pp. 96–7.

Index